Wilderness Wife

Other Collier Books by Bradford Angier:

The Art and Science of Taking to the Woods
(with C. B. Colby)

At Home in the Woods (with Vena Angier)

Food from the Woods Cooking

Home in Your Pack

How to Stay Alive in the Woods

We Like It Wild

Wilderness Gear You Can Make Yourself

Bradford & Vena Angier

Wilderness Wife

Collier Books
A Division of Macmillan Publishing Co., Inc.
New York

*For our original sourdough fellows still in and around Hudson
Hope—Larry and Vesta Gething, Joe and Claire Barkley, the
Ardills, Bakers, Beatties, Blairs, Matt and Erna Boe, Campbells,
Chapples, Bob Clarke, Ellises, Fells, Garbitts, Hamiltons,
Krugers, Kyllos, MacDougalls, Ohlands, Pecks, Pickells, Pollons,
Powells, Robisons, Rutledges, Ray and Frances Sandy, Tomkins,
Wegens, and later-comer Michael John Richmond, as well as our
other friends and neighbors on the Peace River.*

Copyright © 1976 by Bradford and Vena Angier

Macmillan Publishing Co., Inc.
866 Third Avenue, New York, N.Y. 10022
Collier Macmillan Canada, Ltd.

Wilderness Wife was originally published
by Chilton Book Company.

Library of Congress Cataloging in Publication Data
Angier, Bradford.
    Wilderness wife.
    1.   Country life—British Columbia.   2.   Outdoor
life—British Columbia.   3.   Angier, Vena.
4.   Angier, Bradford.   5.   British Columbia—
Biography.   I.   Angier, Vena, joint author.
II.   Title.
S522.C2A53   1977   971.1'1   76-49489
ISBN 0-02-058230-7

First Collier Books Edition 1977

Printed in the United States of America

Contents

1

We Take to the Woods

Thin distant cheeps of migrating birds caught at us, along with
subarctic cold, as we stepped into the British Columbia night.
Wild wings flapped nearer. Raucous cries, mingling vaguely with
the insistence of slush that gave a pewter gleam to the river, all at
once emphasized the smells of approaching winter.

Suddenly, an uneven angle hyphened itself against a sky tremulous with Northern Lights. Wild swan! Spellbound after too
many years in cities, Brad and I stood together and watched the
great swift shapes until they chalked out of sight.

A timber wolf began howling in one of the dry canyons across
the Peace River. The answering bark of our dog was engulfed as

the whole pack joined in, so close that the pandemonium seemed to come from no particular direction but to sound stereophonically all round the clearing. In the wind-heaving stillness that followed, a coyote yipped in the mountains behind us.

Bushman started barking again inside the cabin, his body making leaping shadows in the light from the windows. Only then did I realize that snow was beginning to swirl in our faces. Big soft flakes, heavy as damp feathers, eddied after us into the suddenly wonderful warmth of our newest log home.

"Sorry?" I asked Brad. "Sorry we're here with all the food, the wood, and all the everything else we'll need all winter?"

"Sure, I'm sorry," my husband said, one hand around me and the other stroking the Irish wolfhound's gray head. "I'm sorry we didn't make the break a lot sooner."

Food, warmth, clothing, and shelter: the four necessities! Brad and I had them all, plus such luxuries as saddle horses in the nearby pole corral and shelves of books there was time to read. Especially important here, we had each other. Glancing through the sifting whiteness, where lamplight glistened on stacks of poplar and split pine, I stirred the fire with more satisfaction than ever.

Most of our lives, up to now, we had never been fully happy because we had always wanted to be somewhere else. But, then, isn't this same urge experienced by millions? We all hope some day to answer it. In most cases, though, the desire keeps opening a deeper void in our lives. Our own personal difficulty had been that the quest had led us in what was, for us at least, precisely the wrong direction: toward big cities.

There is one thing I wish we had realized sooner. It's that most of us are working harder than we want, at things we don't like to do. Why? So as to afford the sort of existence we don't care to lead.

Just for example, how about you? Would you rather live where wild fruits and vegetables are free for the picking, trout for the fishing, steak for the hunting, fuel for the cutting, water for the carrying, and a home for the satisfaction of building?

So would we. The only difference between us and a lot of other people, as a matter of fact, is that this is exactly what we seem to be doing.

The word *wilderness* had rung inside Brad early, had welled like the vibrations of a great bell, had eventually filled the whole of his subconscious being. He had not been possessed instantly by a sensate and demanding need to go into the farther places and live with today's pioneers. It was subtler than that, an effect first not of decision but of restlessness.

He gradually realized that something was vaguely, yet definitely, wrong with his life. He began taking longer and longer hunting, fishing and camping leaves of absence from his Boston job as advertising executive and motion picture trade paper correspondent and editor. His Back Bay life became progressively more constrained. What was worse, not one of his friends shared his viewpoint. More and more they seemed to him to be following a meaningless existence, content with frivolity and mediocrity, consumed by a nervous tension which he no longer found bearable.

Eventually that day arrives when you stop and take stock. Life, you sense, is about to change. Something is going to happen. And it does; you have made your decision. This comes to individuals in different ways: Brad's after a damp, desolate walk in a Boston snowstorm. He was drying off in the heated darkness of the Metropolitan Theater, where by virtue of his job he had a pass, still trying to get things straight.

It was in the theater that one of those small things happened that, although scarcely touching you at all, can change the whole trend of your existence. He was sitting there, watching a picture he can't remember, when a man started up the aisle. His step was unsteady. Brad thought: maybe when this stranger had been his age he had wanted to go to the woods, too, and had also kept putting it off. Then he passed Brad's seat and my husband saw he was very old. If the man ever did have such dreams, Brad realized, now it was too late. He decided then and there. He was going to go now.

All that remained was to convince me. Even though I'd seldom been outside the clamor of a big city, that was not difficult. He promised that I was to consider it a one-year honeymoon, after which I was to make up my own mind about where we would live. One year stretched happily into four. The only reason we finally returned to the metropolis was that Brad felt increasingly guilty about having "talked" me into dwelling away from so many "comforts."

Now we were back on the far northern headwaters of the Peace River once more: this time the decision was definitely mutual.

2

Rocky Mountain Canyon

It had been February when Brad and I originally took to the woods. This, I had supposed during the first four years we lived there in a log cabin we built ourselves, had been a matter of chance. But it is generally some time in February, when the snow and the sleet have shut out from the wearied mind even the memory of spring, that the man of the forests generally receives his initial inspiration. So Brad told me after we had been back in the city for several months and it had become February once more.

This calling to the Farther Places? One may hear it in a companion's chance remark, in a vague recollection of a dim-past conservation, sense it from a glance at the map, or a letter with a Canadian stamp bright in the corner, or it may flash on him from the mere pronouncement of a name. The first faint thrill of discovery leaves him cool, but gradually, with increasing enthusiasm, the idea gains body until finally it has grown to proportions fit for discussion.

Of these many quickening potencies of inspiration, the bare name of a place seems to strike deepest at the heart of romance. Color, mystery, the vastness of unexplored space are there, symbolized compactly for nourishment of the imagination. It lures the fancy as a black gnat fly lures the trout. Dawson Creek, Great Bear Lake, Pouce Coupe, Lac La Martre, Finlay Forks, Fort Vermilion, Kluane, Conjuror's House, Hudson Hope—how the syllables roll from the tongue; what pictures rise in instant response to their suggestion! A journey of a thousand miles seems not too great a price for the sight of country called the Land of Little Sticks, for acquaintance with the people who dwell there, perhaps for a glimpse of the sage-spirit that so named its environment. On the other hand, one might feel little desire to visit Mickel Corners, even though at his crossing he were assured of the deepest essence of the Far North.

The initial response to the red god's summons is almost invariably the production of a fly book and the complete rearrangement of its Brown Hackles, Royal Coachmen and other contents. The next is a resumption, perhaps in a muffled city cellar, of practice with the little .22. The third and last is pen and notebook: lists of grub and duffle; estimates of routes and expenses; correspondence with men who spell queerly, bear down heavily with blunt pencils, and agree to be at an Alaska Highway turnoff on a certain date. Now, although the February snow and sleet shut us in, spring had drawn very near. We could feel the warmth of her breath rustling through our reviving memories.

There are said to be sixty-eight roads to heaven, of which but one is the true way. Here and there a bypath offers experimental variety to the restless and bold. This time, though, one definite spot called us—Hudson Hope, British Columbia, where we had been so happy before.

More and more the Far North exerted its pull. It was the clamor of birds wending northward, free as air, that made us sit up soberly one city night and take final stock.

"If a man does not keep pace with his companions, perhaps it is because he hears a different drummer." Distant throaty cries sounded hoarsely against a background of restless city movement. "Let him step to the music which he hears, however measured or far away."

The clangor of the departing birds made me suddenly afraid, perhaps because it blended with impressions of a river which I knew must now be bright with ice cakes, of poplar buds suddenly bursting open on warm mornings with the noise of popcorn, and of grass and wild fruits and vegetables flaming up like a spring fire—as if the earth were sending forth an inward heat to greet the returning sun. I wanted again "to live deep and suck out all the marrow of life." I throbbed, too, to be once more as free as air. Desperately, I ached to return to our home in the woods before something might happen to prevent us.

"We need the tonic of wildness—to wade sometime in marshes

where the bittern and meadow hen lurk, and hear the booming of snipe; to smell the whispering sedge where only some wilder and more solitary fowl builds her nest, and the mink crawls with its belly close to the ground."

The words struck like a precisely inked rubber stamp against a still unwritten page of our lives, and it was as if there drifted through the apartment the pleasant stench of wood smoke that had never entirely escaped from our woolens. More than ever, I realized the truth of what Henry Thoreau had written over a century before; I felt the almost frightened urge to hurry.

"We can never have enough of nature." It seemed as if time was moving inexorably past us, along with the disappearing birds, although Thoreau's sentences seemed to enclose it momentarily like a frame. "We must be refreshed by the sight of inexhaustible vigor, vast and titanic features, the wilderness with its living and decaying trees, the thundercloud, the rain."

Like one who suddenly realizes she's been lost a long time, I wanted to run. When I tried to speak, my voice was uncertain. A lot of memories came crowding back, poignant and clear as the bars of a remembered tune. I found myself trying to shut them off, struggling to put my mind on something impersonal: the present noise of Commonwealth Avenue traffic, the way a passing automobile spread rivulets of light across the plastered ceiling.

"Brad?" I said when I could more nearly trust my voice. I waited for him to answer me. "Brad, don't you feel it, too?"

"Yes," he said finally. "But I always have, for myself." And then he waved an arm. "Here you don't have to scrub clothes, or get your hands sticky with pine pitch, or walk five miles for mail, or . . ."

I drew a quick breath. It was almost a sob and I bit at my lips to steady them.

"Brad," I interrupted, whispering because of the lump in my throat, "don't you want . . . ?" My voice broke and I found myself reaching for him. When he held me against him, I realized my cheek was wet with tears. "Don't you want to go home, too, Brad?"

The way he held me took my thoughts back to those decisive days four years before. I still couldn't speak. Then other words filled the choked silence; words strangely vehement, for the arms about me were so soothing.

"Sure, Vena," he said, almost harshly. "Sure, I feel it. But I practically forced you into going once. I didn't ever want to do that again, not now that you were able from experience to decide for yourself. Besides . . . well, I still don't understand how Thoreau went wrong. He must have been wrong in **leaving** the woods when all that meant so much to him. Yet he was so right in everything else."

"But he was never really wrong, not in real life. That's where we made our mistake." I managed to smile, and lifted my face. His questioning lips met mine, warm and alive. "Thoreau left his cabin on the pond, yes. He didn't mention the rest of it in that book we have, but I've finally been reading more about him as we always said we would."

"What do you mean?" Brad asked.

"Thoreau moved only as far as Concord, where he used to walk regularly from his cabin, anyway," I said. "He spent the rest of his life roaming about the same woods, the same fields and the same Walden Pond."

So Brad and I returned to Hudson Hope, whose two dozen log cabins seemed not to have changed, clustered restfully as they were about one of the red-roofed fur trading posts of the three-century-old Hudson's Bay Company.

A small herd of horses, which I knew had been keeping themselves fat off the country all winter, feeding on snow-buried hay, legumes and other vegetation, whinnied at us from a greening hillside. I walked up to Cloud as I always could; then Brad, with a tempting handful of vetch, managed to entice the warier Chinook. We eased our belts around their necks to lead them. At the Gethings' we picked up our saddlery and, although everyone seemed as glad to see us as we were to be with them again, they understandingly did not seek to delay us now.

We rode the five miles, past our lone neighbor, trapper Dudley Shaw, who lived halfway up the lone trail that followed the sunny north bank of the Peace River into Rocky Mountain Canyon. It was an exquisite moment when our little log cabin, undisturbed although we had left it unlocked, shone into view.

"Here we are, darling," Brad was saying delightedly, as hooves drew platinum splashes from the brook that, a few feet further along, plummeted in a still partially frozen waterfall to the wilderness river some eighty feet below. He grasped Cloud's bridle while I swung to the ground. "Here we are, back home."

An oil lamp was once more our electricity, a pair of pails our water system. There were other inconveniences, too. Well, maybe some people would call them that. We'd thought so, too, before we understood they're also freedoms. If you don't have running water, there's no worry about meters and bursting pipes. If stoves crackle with your own wood, high fuel costs and labor-management difficulties are something to plague the other fellow.

"Here," I heard Brad say almost shyly. I saw he was extending an oblong fold of paper toward me with one hand, while with the other he slipped Cloud's halter rope from my saddle horn. "Here's what I've been trying to get for you ever since that first Christmas here, Vena. It came awhile back, but I figured this would be the right time to give it to you."

"The Fractional South East quarter of the Fractional South East quarter of Lot one hundred and forty-nine, Peace River District," I read, eyes darting from the brilliant red seal in the lower right hand corner to the black Old English lettering at the top, "Certificate of Indefeasible Title."

"It's really ours now, just as you always wanted, this land along the river on both sides of Bull Creek." He motioned with a hand. "I finally managed to buy it from the Provincial Government. It cost five dollars an acre."

3
Lying Awake at Night

Once every so often you lie awake at night. Why this is so I've never been able to discover. It apparently doesn't come from any predisposition to indigestion, too much tea or coffee, or the excitation of an unusual incident or stimulating conversation. Although this was the first night in months that we had crawled into our sleeping bags in our log home, it was as if we had never left. As a matter of fact, I had turned in with the expectation of a rather good night's rest.

Almost at once the little noises of the forest grow larger, blending in the hollow bigness of that first drowse; your thoughts drift idly back and forth between reality and dream when—snap!— you are wide awake. Perhaps the reservoir of your vital forces is so full it overflows; or perhaps, more subtly, Nature insists thus that you enter the temple of her larger mysteries.

For, unlike mere insomnia, lying awake at night in the wilderness is pleasant. The eager, nervous straining for sleep gives way to a delicious indifference. You do not care. Your mind is cradled in an exquisite poppy-suspension of judgment and of thought. Impressions slip vaguely into your consciousness and, just as obscurely, out again. Sometimes they stand naked and stark for your inspection; sometimes they lose themselves in the mist of half sleep. Always they lay soft velvet fingers on the drowsy imagination, so that in their caresses you feel the vaster spaces from which they have come. To hear, to see, to smell: all our senses are preternaturally keen to whatever sound and sight and woods perfume is abroad through the darkness. Yet at the same time, active appreciation dozes, so these things lie on it sweet and cloying like fallen wild rose petals.

In such circumstances—for me, it was against the heavy breathing of Brad and the occasional twitching of Bushman, who lay stretched on the plank floor between our two bunks—you will hear what the sourdoughs call the voices of the rapids. Many people never hear them at all. They speak very softly, low and distinct beneath the steady roar and dashing, beneath even the lesser tinklings and gurglings whose quality superimposes them over the louder sounds. They are like tear forms swimming across the field of vision, disappearing quickly when you concentrate your sight to look at them and reappearing magically when again your gaze turns vacant. In the stillness of your half consciousness they speak. When you bend your attention to listen, they are gone; only the rushings and the tumults remain.

But when you can hear them at all, they are very distinct. Just as an odor will often wake up all of a vanished memory, so these voices—by the force of a large impressionism—suggest whole scenes. Far off are the cling-clang-cling of chimes and the swell and fall of a multitude en *fête*, so that subtly you feel the gray old town with its walls, the crowded marketplace, and decent peasant crowd, the booths, the mellow church building with its ivy and bells, the warm dust-moted sun.

In the pauses between the swish-dash-dashings of the waters, sound faint and clear voices singing intermittently French-Canadian songs, far calls, and distant notes of laughter, as though many freight canoes were working against the current—only the flotilla never gets any nearer, nor the voices any louder. The sourdoughs call these mist people the ghosts of long-departed voyageurs and they look a little frightened. To each is his vision, according to his experience. The nations of the earth whisper to their exiled sons in this New World through the voices of the rapids. Curiously enough, by all reports, they suggest always peaceful scenes: a harvest field, a street fair, a Sunday morning in a cathedral town; never the turmoils and struggles. Perhaps this is great Nature's compensation for a harsh mode of life.

Nothing is more fantastically unreal to talk about, nothing more concretely real to experience, than this undernote of quick water. And when you do lie awake at night, it is always making its unobtrusive appeal. Gradually its hypnotic spell works. The distant chimes ring louder and nearer, as you cross the borderland of sleep. And then outside the cabin some little woods noise snaps the thread. An owl hoots, a loon cries, a twig cracks beneath the cautious prowl of some night creature. At once the yellow sunlit European meadows puff away, and you are staring at the blurred image of the moon spraying through your breath-opaqued windows.

The voices of the rapids have dropped into the background, as have the dashing noises of the brook just outside our door and the thunder of the Peace River below. Through the lodgepole pine forest there is a great silence, but no stillness at all. The whippoorwill swings down and up the short curve of his regular song. Over and over again, two hunting owls say their rapid whoo-whoo-whoos. These, with the ceaseless dash of the rapids, are the webs, upon which the night traces her more delicate embroideries of the unexpected.

Distant crashes, single and impressive; stealthy footsteps near at hand; a faint sniff, sniff, sniff, of inquiry; the sudden, clear ko-ko-ko-oh of the little owl; the mournful, drawn-out call of the loon, indistinct with the spirit of loneliness; the ethereal notes of the birds of passage high in the air; a patter, patter among last fall's dead poplar leaves, immediately stilled; and then at the last, from a serviceberry thicket close at hand, the platinum purity of the white-throated sparrow—the nightingale of the North—trembling as though a shimmering moonbeam had turned to sound; and all the while the blurred figure of the moon mounting over the ridgepole of your log cabin. These things combine subtly until at last the great Silence of which they are a part overarches the night and draws you forth to contemplation.

No beverage is more gratefully drunk than the cup of icy water from Bull Creek, fed by springs three miles inland at the base of Bullhead Mountain; no moment more refreshing than that when your dog is soundlessly at your side and you look about you at the darkened forest. A coolness, physical and spiritual, bathes you from head to foot. All your senses are keyed to the last vibration. You hear the little night prowlers; you glimpse the greater ones. I grasped Bushman's collar, willing him not to bark and disturb Brad, as a moose crashed away.

A faint, searching woods perfume of dampness greets your nostrils. Mysteriously, in a manner not to be understood, the forces of the world seem in suspension, as though a touch might crystallize infinite possibilities into infinite power and motion. But the touch lacks. The forces hover on the edge of action, unmindful of the little noises. In humbleness and awe, you are once more a dweller of the Silent Places.

At such a time, you will relive past adventures. One night, on the wild Half Moon of the Southwest Miramichi River in New Brunswick, Brad routed eight salt-hungry porcupines from his overturned canoe. On gold-rich Mount Selwyn, near where the Finlay and Parsnip Rivers meet to form the mighty Peace, we once discovered seven mountain sheep cropping the herbage like so many beautiful ghosts. A prospecting friend, across on the Wicked River, tells us of a moose calf that every night used to sleep outside his tent, within a foot of his head, probably by way of protection against timber wolves. Its mother had in all likelihood been killed. The instant our friend moved toward the tent opening, the gangling little creature would disappear; it was always gone by earliest daylight.

Nocturnal bears, lured by the smell of camp bacon, are not uncommon. But even though your imagination meets nothing but the bats and the woods shadows and the Northern Lights, those few moments of the sleeping world comprise a physical experience to be gained in no other way. You cannot know the wilderness night by sitting up; she will sit up with you. Only by coming into her presence from the borders of sleep can you meet her face to face in the intimate mood.

The night wind from the river and from the open spaces of the wilds chills you after a time. You begin to think of your goose-down sleeping robe. In a few moments you draw its soft kersey flap up around your face. Instantly it is morning.

And, strange to say, you have not to pay by going through the next day unrefreshed. You may feel, as I did, like turning in at nine o'clock instead of ten and you may fall asleep with unusual promptitude, but your day will begin clear-headedly, proceed bouncily, and end with much in reserve. No languor, no dull headache, no exhaustion follows your experience. For once, your three hours of sleep have been as effective as eight.

4

Food for the Gathering

One of the major attractions of coming back to the woods was that we could begin living off the country again. Not only does this save money, but the pleasure of eating and nutritional values derived from foods are greatly increased.

Green leafy vegetables, to give just one example, deteriorate very rapidly. Even when purchased as fresh as obtainable from the most conscientious nearby market, they'll already have lost a sizable proportion of their vitamins. Some of the food values of greens diminish as much as one third during the first hour after picking. But gather them fresh from nature's own garden and eat them when they are at their tastiest. You'll enjoy the best they have to offer.

That was why, when Brad asked me the next morning, "What would you like to do, darling, on our first full day back in the woods?" I was ready with my answer.

"Let's put a pack on Bushman, take a lunch, and see what wild foods we can find."

"Great," he said. "I'll take the .22. From the looks of things, this is close to being another peak rabbit year and we'll need some meat to go along with those greens. Don't forget the tea pail."

Few of the American and Canadian Indians had gardens when Columbus rediscovered the New World. Instead, they regularly supplemented their meat and fish with wild fruits, nuts, roots, tubers, greens, seeds, beverages and the like, which they gathered free from the land. You and I can have the satisfaction of doing the same thing today, for these edible wild plants grow everywhere. Especially during trying periods of inflation and unemployment, gourmets, campers and stay-at-home cooks alike will find pleasure in harvesting their meals from the wild lands where nature is the farmer and where nothing is ever due at any checkout counter.

"Oh, I forgot my leather gloves," I said after we'd walked inland about half a mile.

"That's all right, I've got mine," Brad said, reaching into a pocket. "Found some nettles, have you?"

There they were, single-stemmed and dark green. The opposite pairs of leaves were coarsely veined, ranging from egg shaped to oblong, with heart-like bases, rough and sharply toothed. Both the young stem and leaf surfaces already bristled with a fuzz of numerous, fine prickles containing irritating formic acid. Brad, gloves on and knife out, began filling a paper bag.

"Ummm," I enthused, knowing that protein-rich nettles are among the most versatile and potentially valuable of all plants.

In some parts of the world you can sleep between nettle sheets, eat off a nettle tablecloth and dine on nettle-enriched steak and eggs ordered from a nettle-paper menu. In an emergency, you can fish with a nettle line and, in the springtime especially, revel with delectable nettle dishes washed down with nettle beer. In fact, these are only a few of the capabilities of these wild edibles which thrive from Alaska across Canada, south throughout most of the U.S. Incidentally, their presence is usually a good sign that the ground is fertile.

"There," Brad said at last, stowing the bag in our Irish wolfhound's pack. "What next?"

"Back when I was a kid in New England," I said, "my grandmother would have been looking for cowslips this time of year."

He threw an arm about me.

"Sorry," he said, "no cowslips this far north in British Columbia." He brightened. "But there are fiddleheads both places. When I was going to college in Maine, there was so many young ostrich ferns in the spring that some of the Lewiston markets carried big boxes of them. There's a good stand of bracken on that dry, sunny bluff just above the moose lick straight ahead."

We passed some flowering, kitten-whiskered pussy willows as we followed Bull Creek toward the first bluffs, the foothills of the Canadian Rockies. Then there was a lamblike bleat and a cow moose crashed away from the mineral-salty lick, followed by two tiny tan calves.

"Heel," Brad called with sudden sharpness and Bushman obediently stood quivering behind us.

Lifting singly from stout, black, widely spreading roots, brown masses of last year's pasture brakes—the commonest of this continent's ferns—pointed up the presence below them of emerging fiddleheads.

"Five to six inches tall," Brad said, picking one and rubbing off the silvery gray hair between his palms before handing it to me. "Just right. Try one raw, Vena."

I found it pleasant and mucilaginous, although I prefer fiddleheads cooked.

"Aren't they supposed to be bad for you raw?" I asked.

"Not unless you eat too many," Brad said. "That's because of the enzyme thiaminase, which, attacks vitamin B_1 in our bodies when you eat a lot of fiddleheads. Cooking destroys the harmful enzyme, though. That's something to remember if you're ever lost and hungry."

Young fiddleheads, which are the edible parts above ground, are good when they're anywhere from about four to ten inches tall, depending on the locality. Called fiddleheads because of a resemblance in this emerging stage to the tuning ends of violins, they are also known in some places as croziers because of their likeness to the shepherds' crooklike staffs of abbots, bishops and abbesses. The three sections of the leaf later uncoil, like an opening eagle's claw, on their way to toughening and becoming poisonous to cattle as well as humans.

This particular genus with only one species, *Pteridium aquilinum*, is cosmopolitan and widely spread over North America, from Alaska and Labrador southward, as it is in many areas of the world. At home in most places, although rarely in the rich and moist locales so typical of many ferns, it is found in full sunlight in woods, old pastures, new roadsides, burned-over regions, sandy and partially shaded areas, and in thickets.

"There," Brad said at last. "That should be plenty. I'd had fiddleheads in the past in New Brunswick. There the Indians still make a good deal of money gathering the shoots of the ostrich fern in the spring. Back in 1783 this wild food kept the Loyalists from starving to death."

Now Bushman's pack, which lay across the front part of his back, bulged on both sides. He was watching the zigzagging flight of a varying hare longingly although, now that he was working, he visibily quelled his instinct to chase it.

"We may as well wait until we're headed home before I collect our meat," Brad said. "The rabbits are everywhere this year, aren't they? See—you can tell how deep the snow got in here by how high they nibbled on those willows!"

"I'm getting sort of hungry right now," I said. "Nothing like fresh air for the appetite. When do you want to boil the kettle?"

"Let's get a mess of dandelions first," he said. "There are bound to be some in that clearing where they cut the logs for the town church a few years ago. We can get our water there, too."

There's hardly a month in the year, except in winter, when you can't find the golden smile of the dandelion. Sometimes you can even find it when snow's on the ground. It's probably the best-known flower in the world, if often the least appreciated. Ever notice how the big yellow blossoms, frequently the first wild flowers to foretell the spring and one of the last to remain in the fall, are composed of numerous, individual, tiny flower tubes, each broadening into a slim long strap? The golden tubes are arranged on a round disk with the straps extending in a circle, those at the edges unfurling first.

Because these yellow petals are like the golden teeth of the lion of heraldry, there is some dispute as to whether they or the toothed leaves are responsible for the French cognomen, *dent de lion*, from which the English name has been slurred. It is interesting that in almost every European country the local name means the same thing. The humble and beautiful dandelion has followed man abundantly to almost every inhabited corner of Canada and the United States.

"Oh, there're plenty," I said, reaching a clearing surrounded by tall spruces.

We pick dandelions differently from most people. This plant, which has saved whole populations from starvation, is a three-tiered food: the succulent roots, the tender and tasty crowns, and the tops—from the young leaves to the flower buds—are all exceptionally tasty and sustaining.

What a meal we had that night after a hunger-rousing day in the open! Scraped and sliced, then boiled in salted water, the dandelion roots were not only of pleasant taste and texture but also, probably because we hadn't enjoyed any for a year, surprisingly sweet. The rest of the plant, started in bubbling water, had a clean bitterish tang.

The dark green nettles, which I dropped into salted boiling water and then removed from the heat, were tender almost immediately and ready for a crowning pat of margarine as soon as they were cool enough to eat. Don't overcook your wild vegetables. We like the sweetish fiddleheads, which I find reminiscent of okra, simmered in a little salted water until tender, then salted and peppered to taste and eaten hot with plenty of melting margarine.

Everything was set off by the fried varying hare. Here, in case you are interested, is our favorite way of cooking America's most hunted game. Divide the rabbit or hare into serving pieces, disjointing whenever possible. Dip each portion in milk. Salt and pepper, then roll lightly in flour.

Put one-half stick of margarine or butter and four tablespoons of cooking oil in a heavy frypan over high heat. Put in the pieces, any bony sides uppermost. Lower the temperature at once and cook, uncovered, until the portions are brown on one side. Then turn just once and brown the other side. The meat will be crisp and done in slightly more than half an hour. Spread it out on absorbent paper and keep it warm while concocting the gravy.

Pour out all the fat except enough to just cover the bottom of the frypan. Stir in two tablespoons of flour, one-half teaspoon of salt, and one-eighth teaspoon of freshly ground black pepper, smoothing these into a paste. Using the milk in which you immersed the meat, add additional milk to make a cupful. Pour this, then a cup of water, slowly into the pan, all the time stirring. Simmer over low heat for twelve minutes, adding more milk and water if the gravy becomes too thick. Finally, sprinkle with paprika and parsley flakes. With everything served hot, the gravy has enough distinctiveness to transmute fried wild rabbit into an art form.

As the sun sank below a horizon of deep delphinium blue, we found ourselves savoring the almost painfully delicious food deliberately, mouthful by exquisite mouthful.

5

Another Log Cabin

The Hudson Hope wilderness had never looked so beautiful as it did that spring and summer. It seemed to be in an almost desperate mood to unfurl its wonders as a climaxing temptation to remain untouched or, failing that, as a final spendthrift offering to a thankless civilization.

"Progress" was threatening the Peace River. There had been serious talk of this before when the Canadian Pacific sought an economic way to extend its railway lines through the northern mountains. The company had sent survey crews throughout the pass, where the river still cut serenely from west to east through the backbone of the Canadian Rockies. But nothing came of that and the population of this huge northeastern portion of unspoiled British Columbia remained about one human being—white man or Indian—for every twelve and a half square miles.

Now hordes of company-employed prospectors in fleets of helicopters invaded this previously unmapped vastness—a wilderness formerly seen by only a few far-flung trappers and solitary gold panners. Scientific bands accompanied by surveyors hacked their way everywhere, until Brad and I no longer felt easy swimming and bathing nude—as we had, untroubled, for years—in the refreshing coolness below our once lonely reef. The long roller-coaster dirt road between Hudson Hope and the Alaska Highway, and the one across river from Moberly Lake, to the new Hart Highway between Prince George and Dawson Creek, were so improved that the trim little Hudson's Bay Company outpost in Hudson Hope closed. Its trade had been absorbed by the expanded H.B.C. store in now booming Fort St. John, fifty miles downriver. There was more and more talk about damming Rocky Mountain Canyon where, except for a solitary neighbor, we had always lived alone.

Brad and I had more and more misgivings about the unknown future, grounded on the realization that the known was no longer impregnable. The growing whiff of doubt had formerly been too delicate to analyze, akin to steering a small boat up through rapids when some change of timing in the all-important outboard motor communicates itself to you for a will-o'-the-wisp instant, then is lost amid the rush of water.

"We've fought so hard to escape civilization," I said to Brad one afternoon while getting water from our brook. The afternoon sun slanted yellow into my eyes. "Is it going to follow us here? The government has always seemed so steadfast in guarding this wilderness."

"*Sed quis custodiet ipsos custodes?*" Brad queried.

"What does that mean? I never was much good at Latin."

"Who guards the guardians?"

Bushman began barking.

"Someone's coming," Brad said.

All of a sudden the simpler days when a rain barrel meant soap, and a flour barrel spelled bread, seemed a long way off.

The visitor's card identified him as Victor J. Wiebe, senior land representative of the British Columbia Hydro and Power Authority, and soon we were all sipping tea from our stainless steel cups, cool as porcelain. Mr. Wiebe was as nice as he could be, but the point was that if we refused to sell, the government would take our land by eminent domain.

"But we planned to spend the rest of our lives here," I tried to explain. "This is just the place we've always wanted. If you knew all the trouble we had getting here!"

"We're taking all that into consideration in the price we're offering you," Wiebe said regretfully, "although I realize that some things are beyond a monetary value."

"This seems to be a strange place to dam the Peace River," Brad said.

"The main dam will be at the head of the Canyon," Wiebe said. "B.C. Hydro plans a second, smaller, power dam here. It's all been checked very carefully."

After all, there was nothing we could do.

We had become intimately associated with the wild Peace River. It started as the Finlay and Parsnip Rivers in the Continental Trough, flowed from west to east through the entire breadth of the Rocky Mountains, thence to Great Slave Lake in the Northwest Territories. There it became the Mackenzie River and proceeded to the Arctic Ocean.

This wilderness thoroughfare was navigable for its entire 2200 miles, except for the 22-mile stretch through Rocky Mountain Canyon where we lived. Even Sir Alexander Mackenzie had to portage around this canyon when in 1793 he became the first of all explorers, after 301 years of failure, to cross North America north of Mexico. Brad and I were the only people to live in this tumultuous fastness except for a single neighbor, fur trapper and H.B.C. summer clerk Dudley Shaw, whose lone cabin was two and a half miles downriver, exactly halfway between our log cabin and town.

We didn't want to leave the otherwise unfrequented Rocky Mountain Canyon with its shale cliffs festooned with thousands of gourdlike cliff swallow nests, its vast moose yards, its 180-pound timber wolves, its kinnikinic-greened slopes bared in winter by chinooks, and the elusive beauty of the towering coal-streaked mass around which it wound. Timbered Bullhead Mountain, a landmark from the Alaska Highway but invisible from Hudson Hope itself and from our cabin, loomed startlingly into view again once we'd climbed the slope beyond the dry canyons and beaver meadows across river or had ascended the winding Peace another two miles.

We admired this canyon where we dwelled, as Thoreau had put it, "like a corolla in its calyx, like an acorn in its cup. Here, of course," he had added, "is all you love, all that you expect, all that you are."

November arrived, and with it came the time to move. We were relieved—if, at the same time, regretful—that Dudley, who had reached his seventies, decided to build a small home in town. For the price we got for our Bull Creek homesite, we bought Dudley Shaw's cabin and fifty surrounding acres, two and a half miles upriver from Hudson Hope. Here, just west of the historic Peace River Block Line, we continued to live in our beloved Rocky Mountain Canyon, now its only inhabitants.

Brad and I thereby became builders again. As Thoreau had said, and as we had earlier proved to our own satisfaction, "There is some of the same fitness in a man's building his own house that there is in a bird building its own nest. Who knows but if men constructed their own dwelling with their own hands, and provided food for themselves and family simply and honestly enough, the poetic faculty would be universally developed, as birds universally sing when they are so engaged."

"Thoreau was right," Brad said now, slitting with his knife the wrapper of a heavy roll of asphalt-impregnated paper. "Shall we forever resign the pleasure of construction to the carpenter?" our mentor had mused.

We had Dudley's solid little twelve-by-sixteen-foot cabin as a nucleus, but our friend had lived in it as a bachelor, which made a difference. For one thing, following the custom of the North Country, his home had only two tiny windows: one in the east wall, where the morning sun could greet him except in the winter; the other, equally small, on the south side where there was a glorious view across and up the Peace River.

"How could he possibly live here with just two little windows?" I asked Brad, "especially as there's the best scenery here of any place on the river?"

"Dudley figured that when he wanted to look at the view, he could step outdoors," my husband informed me seriously. "In the meantime, like a lot of other sourdoughs, he was saving firewood by having as few openings as possible."

"If you'll fell the wood, I'll help you skid it in with Cloud and Chinook," I promised. "Then after you split it, I'll do the stacking. I'll gladly help carry it in, too. But I just can't live with such miniscule windows, especially not after leaving a cabin with four double windows banked on its south side."

"Neither can I," he said. "I'll have Les Bazely pick up some windows, lumber and more roofing paper in Fort St. John and bring them to town with the next mail. Then we can have Ted Boynton haul them here, along with our winter grubstake."

"Why all the building supplies?"

"We'll want a second room on the west side for storage and the airtight heater, a walk-in cache at the back for meat, plus a whole lot of cabinets and shelves. Besides, you remember Dudley was all the time fighting leaks. We'll need a new double roof over the old one."

I could see that he was right and I laughed at us.

"Why is it," I asked, "that we always seem to be moving and building in the winter?"

"That way," he said reasonably, "we're all ready for the best season in the woods, springtime. I'll catch Les before he leaves with the outgoing mail in the morning. Then we can have everything here in a week."

Everything was. There was such a load that Ted had to leave our grubstake for a second trip. Soon we were learning all over again that hewing your own home out of the wilderness returns one close to the beginning of things. The instinctive hut-building ardor of small children is the proof. Our building project captivated us with such enthusiasm that, except for somewhat reluctant periods of eating and sleeping, we worked almost steadily.

Inasmuch as the common procedure in log cabin construction—about which Brad was writing a book that I was able to illustrate with nearly 150 on-the-spot drawings—is to build solid walls, then later saw out the openings, the new windows were no problem. We first measured everything very carefully inside and out. Then we nailed on perpendicular boards with the assistance of a plumb line (in our case a string, the end weighed down by knotting it to a .22 cartridge) along the inside and outside of each wall where a cut was to be made. These were to guide the saw.

Each cut was started by boring a hole, with a borrowed brace and bit, at the upper corner where each opening was to be made. A keyhole saw, likewise on loan from Ted Boynton, was then inserted through each aperture in turn. A section of the top log was then cut out.

The remainder of the opening was easily made with a big crosscut saw, each of us hauling on one end. Brad then finished framing the window and finally set in the sashes. We made the big, square, four-sash southern window solid; the long two-sash window on the east was made so that one side would slide back and forth. The way the cabin then began warming up was heartening, for the weather was cold by then. With snow streaking across the frozen river, we were working as much as possible with gloved hands.

"How do you like it?" Brad asked expectantly.

"Let's try the furniture first," I suggested.

"All right," he said. "Come on in, Bushman, if you're going to."

We placed our large table in front of the southern expanse of glass and Brad's moosehide-backed straight chair at its eastern end. With a wall-large bank of new shelves at his back, he could type facing upriver.

"What a view!" he exclaimed. "It'll take me awhile to become accustomed enough to it to concentrate."

Showing two and a half more miles of river, the vista was even more spectacular than the one we'd left behind, although the view from our first cabin was splendid. This way, too, I realized, we could enjoy all the golden dazzle of sunshine there was during the shortening winter days.

Directly opposite us was a long wooded island, behind which lifted the familiar shale cliffs of Rocky Mountain Canyon. On this side of the wilderness stream, though, the shore slanted gradually to a broad reef from which we dipped our drinking water. The expanse in here on this side of the Peace was the only spot within miles where you could walk down to the river.

In a southeasterly direction was a second, higher and rockier island where the Canada geese would return to nest in the spring. It was toward the west that the panorama really asserted itself, though. For over three miles, the silver gleam of the river bent in an S curve toward the narrowness of Box Canyon. Beyond it a line of hills, dark with spruce and lodgepole pine, extended across the horizon, broken only at what we have named Starfish Creek, because of the fossils to be found there (the real name of the stream is Deep Creek).

"Magnificent," I echoed.

"Yes," he said, pushing himself to his feet with obvious reluctance. "Well, back to work."

The new log room on the west, in which there was another southern window and in which we set our heater instead of having it, like Dudley's, in the center of the main room floor, went up without difficulty. So did the new watertight roof, which we built an insulated foot above the two-feet-thick old roof for additional warmth. I'd found I could tell which log cabins in Hudson Hope were cozy by walking through the little settlement when the temperature was 30° or more below zero. Escaping heat kept the roofs of the cold homes free of snow.

Then Brad constructed a walk-in cache in back, in which we hung our two remaining deer quarters and several slabs of bear meat. With all the moving, building and getting in cord after cord of dry wood, we still needed to get a moose apiece for the remaining cold weather.

6

Glissade

The snow, which had started the night Brad and I heard both the departing swans and the nearby wolf pack, continued to spit down, sometimes thickly, for the next few weeks. When Ted Boynton finally drove down with our winter's grubstake, his two horses hauled a creaking sleigh. Dudley Shaw had accompanied him with the load of boxes, plump bags and packages. Les Bazely had picked them up for us at the wholesale grocer's in Dawson Creek, by virtue of a special provincial wholesale license that Brad had bought for a few dollars.

Ted was going to take back a load of books and odds and ends for Dudley, along with his old hand-cranked, horn-equipped phonograph. It was so ancient that I almost expected to see the venerable Francis Barraud trademark of a fox terrier listening to it. But Dudley—who, until they knew him better, people saw as a scanty haired, wispy little man with bright chipmunk's eyes and a kind, bony face—regarded it now with a sort of affection. When, by way of greeting, he took my extended hand in both of his, it was with a granite grip.

"That cache of yours is a noble idea," he said in a voice that was not at all small, while Bushman's tail flailed. "I don't know how I got by so many years without one. But, then, a little lap [tea] and some sourdough bread and saskatoon jam pretty much sees me through the winter."

"How are you two fixed for meat this year?" Ted asked us, his button mouth widening in a slow, leathery smile. He was a round man with merry eyes and unruly black hair that a stocking cap only tossed more askew. He must be over sixty years old, I thought, and I knew Dudley was in his late seventies, but neither one had yet started to gray.

"We still have to get our two moose," Brad said, "With building and all, I haven't had a chance to do any hunting except for an odd rabbit."

"Hordes of wapoose this year," Dudley noted.

"Well, the moose season is still open through part of December," Ted said. "I imagine that the game wardens are going to tighten up now that civilization is moving in. Before, as long as I've been here, a man could knock over some of the Queen's beef whenever he was hungry."

"Well, maybe to stretch a point," Brad said, "I still have a Free Miner's Certificate that will let us keep ourselves in meat the year around as long as we're prospecting. Cost me five dollars."

"Perhaps that's what I should get, too," Ted said. "Plenty of color hereabouts. A man can pan himself wages any day."

Puffy mounds of cumulous clouds were streaming from northwest to southeast by the time Dudley and Ted, regretting that they had a job back in town that wouldn't let them stay for lunch, had pulled back up the trail toward Hudson Hope. Snowflakes wafted down through the golden glitter of sunlight for about half an hour, then stopped entirely. The food supply put away, neither of us wanted to stay indoors any longer.

"Let's build a fire down on the ledge and eat there," I urged.

"All right," Brad said instantly, as if he'd been thinking along the same lines. "I'll take the pails and the ax, too, and then we can bring up our water on the way back. Better fetch that deer bone for Bushman."

It was wonderful to be eating outdoors again. We sat in a cleared spot on the smooth ledge, upwind of the smoke and just above the frozen river, toasting thick peanut butter and raspberry jam sandwiches on green willow wands, while the water in the blackened tea pail commenced its leaping bubble. For a long time after the last of the food was gone and we were sharing the strong black H.B.C. Fort Garry tea, my husband remained motionless, his arms clasped about his long legs and his blue eyes squinting upriver.

He was still looking up the river that evening at dinner time, now from his seat at the table by the big windows. The last light of the afternoon slanted through, sun-warmed and wind-cold, gleaming and glinting on Bushman's bearskin rug and on the book-crammed shelves behind. A series of Currier and Ives wilderness prints eyed each other benevolently from opposite walls. From my kitchen corner a clattering of chinaware, along with the crackling of the softwood fire and a stuttering cover on a pot of mulligan, filled the small room with sound; I moved back and forth from the heat to the comparative coolness with dishes and stainless steel knives, forks and spoons.

With the fine weather showing every sign of continuing, we were going hunting the next day: probably upriver, where I could see the radiant wedge of bluffs that marked the start of Starfish Creek. We had given it this name because a few years previously, our friend King Gething had found starfish fossils here. A government geologist, Dr. Frank H. McLearn, appending *kingi* to their scientific name, had later gratefully accepted them for the Ottawa Museum.

On our little Zenith all-wave radio, which had been giving us the uninspiring news of a world that seemed remote, a faraway orchestra played the slow movement from Beethoven's Emperor Concerto with bittersweet precision.

"I wonder when there'll be another dance in the Hope?" I said.

"It won't ever be the same again," Brad replied. I realized he was right, although here in our obscure niche, even with all the intruding activities of the past few months, it seemed as though we were still in an untouched primitive nook of our own.

"Shall we take the horses?" Brad said the next morning.

There were still shelves and cabinets to build, as well as a working counter for my kitchen in the northeast corner of the cabin by the hot-water well of our big iron stove, but we could do that when the weather was not so fine.

"Don't you feel like walking?" I said. "We've been penned up so much lately."

"All right," he agreed. "I'll go out and throw the cayuses their bundles while you're putting up the lunch."

Once the canvas pack I had sewn for Bushman was filled with

the ingredients of a meal, the Irish wolfhound eagerly thrust his head between the breast strap and the twin sacks. He was so anxious to be on his way that I found it difficult to keep him still long enough to rope the pack in place.

"Shall I take my .250-3000?" I asked Brad when he'd finished his chores and was reaching for his scope-sighted Winchester Model 70 .30-06.

"May as well," he said. "You can never tell when you'll get a chance at something. Didn't forget to put in a tea pail, did you? That's one good thing about snow. We can have a drink wherever we want it."

"I've got everything, I think," I told him.

We walked up the smooth northern edge of the Peace River ice, where overflow had frozen like a winding sidewalk, through the sun-streaked forest to the narrowness of Box Canyon. This soon opened onto a slope-guarded wideness, with blackened saskatoon bushes sticking starkly out of the snow where some tenderfoot cheechako's fire up by the start of the portage had gotten away from him. On this berry-enriched hillside, we had two years before glimpsed six feeding bear during the same afternoon. Up on top now was a charred tangle of fallen trees. Fortunately, however, the fire had not leaped to the south bank and there one could still roam freely among the forest aisles.

It was fun, walking up the open river ice with the sun beating upon our backs. The dark lenses of my sunglasses gave an agreeably cool, greenish aspect to everything. Like Thoreau, I'd early found I had a genius for sauntering, the art of which consisted not only in exercising legs or body, nor solely in recruiting the spirits, "but positively to exercise both body and spirit." Similarly, too, I set forth on these walks with my husband " . . . in the spirit of undying adventure."

Moreover, I found we both reacted to an elusive magnetism in nature that drew us irresistibly in the direction away from town. That's why I was glad this morning when he turned upriver, once more moving west.

"Always Americans have turned west, body and soul," Douglas Culross Peattie says in *The Road of a Naturalist*. "They love the national tradition of unbreathed air, and they welcome a solitude that is not lonely but free."

In the subtle energy of magnetism in nature, Thoreau perceived the general truth of our heading eastward for history,

literature and art, "retracing the steps of the race"—and trending
westward, "as into the future, with a spirit of enterprise and adventure."

He said in *Walden*, and so I thought now: "Our village life
would stagnate if it were not for the unexplored forests and
meadows which surround it. We can never have enough of nature. We must be refreshed by the sight of inexhaustible vigor,
vast and titanic features, the seacoast with its wrecks, the wilderness with its living and decaying trees, the thundercloud, and the
rain."

Bushman, shoulder hair bristling, came across the fresh moose
tracks first, soon after we'd finished boiling the kettle for our
noonday meal. Even I could tell they had just been made. There
was a difference in the color of the snow where they had cut the
surface and the hardened balls from between the hooves had not
yet frozen.

"Oh, may I come with you?" I asked.

"The snow will muffle our movements enough so that it
shouldn't make any difference," he said after a moment, "and
we'll have a better chance for a shot together. You're sure you
won't mind shooting it, though? If we're lucky enough to get it, we
need the meat to live on this winter. None of it will be wasted."

I remembered the usually vegetarian Thoreau once feeling the
powerful impulse to seize and down a woodchuck raw, and I
knew how he must have reasoned. After all, hadn't he written, "I
love to see that Nature is so rife with life that myriads can be af-
forded to be sacrificed and suffered to prey on one another. The
impression made on a wise man is that of universal innocence.
Compassion is an untenable ground. It must be expeditious. Its
pleadings will not bear to be stereotyped."

The tracks climbed an almost sheer slope on the shaded
southern side of the river, just downstream from the mouth of
Starfish Creek. We wound our way up the narrow slipperiness
cautiously, grasping bushes where we could, floundering across
sheer graveled stretches. Panting, we finally emerged on a high,
pine-clasped point and, clearing a space on a sunlit ledge, we sat
to regain our breaths.

From this height, although Hudson Hope itself was hidden, we
could tell where it was by the formation of the hills. My eyes
came back to the spot after following the frozen ribbon of river all
the way to the smokes of Fort St. John on the Alaska Highway. A

truck labored up the series of switchbacks to the portage above the village, giving life to the scene, which the faraway roar of the laboring motor soon confirmed.

We sat for what seemed a long time, while the thrumming of my racing heart quieted. With eyes partially closed against the glare, we gazed at the valley with its toy world and, behind us, at the white wildness of Bullhead Mountain. Afternoon shadows thronged in the depths below and gradually climbed the mountainside. Finally we, too, were in the shade and it grew abruptly cold. But the sun still struck splinters of light from the broad white summit across from us as, wordlessly, we turned into the conifer-scented stillness of the woods.

Ahead of us, somewhere in the dark evergreen and poplar forest, a moose grunted with low, gutteral intensity. Bushman, obediently heeling, quivered with excitement. When the moose oo-waughed again, the dog bounded forward, but Brad managed to catch his pack.

"Heel," he commanded again in a low voice. "Heel, Bushman." Despite his instinctive excitement, the wolfhound obeyed grudgingly.

Even if Brad had not been ahead of me and if the huge dew-clawed tracks had not been at my feet, I could have followed the recent progress of the big animal—one of the largest deer that have ever trod this globe—by the fresh green path he had left through the snow-laden spruce. Then we were out of the denseness, in a parklike expanse of poplar. Brad stopped repeatedly to glass the area ahead with the binoculars that he carried around his neck, buttoned inside his jacket when not in use.

I could see where the animal's progress had lost is directness, where he had nipped the ends from poplar branches higher than I could reach. That made me realize I was hungry again myself and I glanced at my wristwatch. The hour was after three o'clock, near the early northern sunset, but Brad showed no sign of turning back. I realized that the wind had changed.

Sharp pellets of snow started to sting my face. I hunched beneath their lash, apprehensive lest they should fill in the trail. Even inside my goose-down jacket, I shivered. When I glanced back at Bushman, I could see icicles lengthening below his muzzle. We crossed a recent grizzly trail. There the moose had wandered back toward the brink again and I inched away from the sheer, icy drop-off. More thick spruce clawed at me and dropped snow down my neck.

The moose had been feeding into the wind and now he started zigzagging widely. Brad had told me before what that meant, so when he looked back now and held up a cautioning hand, I stopped. The moose was figuring on lying down. There'd be the wind at his back, to protect him, Brad had explained; as for his main trail, he'd be watching that. I stood with Bushman and watched my husband, working crosswind now, circle inland of the imprints, all the time looking.

A tremendous black bulk clambered abruptly upright from a clump of fir fifty feet to my right, apparently out of Brad's sight. He was trotting away with cumbersome speed. Trees were in the way of my sights. Then Bushman burst from behind me and he was at the moose's heels. I was running in that direction, too, my rifle's safety dangerously off, but my forefinger at least cautiously on the trigger guard.

The moose turned at the noise. Bushman hurled himself at his throat and the great black beast—the heaviest wild, meat animal in North America—struck at the dog with savagely flashing forefeet. Bushman, hit, tumbled toward the edge of the bluff. The moose, antlers lowered, was charging after him.

His dark neck filled my sights. My shot resounded before I realized I was squeezing the trigger. The moose staggered, tried to turn and then fell sidewise over the bluff. I was at the edge in time to watch his bounding, skidding fall. He remained a still black heap at the edge of the frozen river, snow trickling after him although the incline here was so steep that it was nearly bare.

Bushman's oxford-gray tail gave a feeble sweep when I fell onto my knees beside him. Brad was with me by this time. We felt the dog's head and front legs without finding anything wrong, but when I reached the ribs over his wildly beating heart he gave a slight yip and licked my hand. We went over the rest of him carefully. When I returned my fingers to the tender spot, he only winced a little bit.

"I guess you mostly got the breath knocked out of you," I said, holding him close in my relief and breathing through his thick wiry hair.

"Well, we got our meat. Now what?"

"Now the work starts," Brad said, arm around me. "But first we've got to get down there."

The squall had passed, but sudden blasts of wind seemed to be shaking this river-rift shoulder of Bullhead Mountain. They roared like explosions, but only lasted seconds at a time, while I clung to a drooping birch with Brad and Bushman close beside me. Then the wind smashed at us from seemingly every direction at once, flinging up icy pellets of snow from the ground.

I made my buffeted way to where the slope was more gradual and there was deeper snow to slow my descent, so I thought. There I set my heels and, leaning on the butt of my now unloaded rifle, started my glissade. I'd practiced these controlled, effortless slides one winter, years before at North Conway, New Hampshire.

Only the heavier snow fooled me. It surged after with increasing thunder. When my boots hit an unexpected projection and I sprawled abruptly forward, out of all control, it engulfed me.

There was a deepening roar and I was tumbling with the great rolling mass, all sense of equilibrium gone. I came to rest on a bottomless mattress, the thud of falling shapes resounding dully on my ears and my wind gone. When I tried to move, to breathe again, to claw my way to safety, I encountered only snow. It pressed upon me with cold, dead heaviness.

7

Grizzly!

Even though everything was now muffled, a tremendous roaring, with crunchings and rumblings that jarred my very bones, still seemed very near. I tried to see, but cold dry snow pressed against my eyes. I tried to breathe, but that was impossible until, with a hand that was blessedly close to my head, I managed to clear a little space in front of my face.

Everything was jamming in toward me; it was as though I were being smothered. For a desperate instant, I tried to shove the tumbled mass of inert coldness away from me, to scream for help, but it was all useless.

The claustrophobic feeling became more and more stifling, although I fought to stay calm. The pressures on my body seemed to be becoming heavier and I could scarcely find enough air to draw into my laboring lungs. The more I struggled to move, the more constricted my heavy silent world became, but I knew Brad must be working to get me out.

The darkness, burdensome as Bullhead Mountain, appeared to have a thousand stifling fists. I felt stranger than I have ever before in my life. Momentary terror poured over me, so hotly that I might have been caught in an ocean of lava instead of icy, unyielding snow. A choked, imponderable resonance was all about me in the pulsing, drumming stillness. I listened to it dully, then realized that threaded through it was Bushman's frantic barking.

Dizzily, I couldn't drag in even one more breath. I felt my senses reeling away. Then, suddenly, living fingers clutched my shoulder and Brad had both hands on me, hauling me into the wonderfully bright, sweet, beautiful sunlight.

"Th-thank you," I said, standing on the river's edge, trembling but desperately happy to be alive.

When the Irish wolfhound surged up between Brad and me to lick my face, I lowered my cheek against his shaggy neck and held him close, too.

"He started digging for you right away," Brad said. "I wasn't sure where to start. Are you all right? Are you hurt?"

"I . . . I seem to be fine," I said shakily, returning his kiss. "At least, the snow was like a cushion."

Down here on the Peace River the wind was subdued. With Brad's help, I brushed myself off. Bushman shook himself clean in a tremendous surge of motion that started at his head and ended at his long oxford-gray tail.

The barrel of my lever-action Savage, when we retrieved it, proved to be clogged with snow. My husband worked a slim willow wand out the muzzle from the chamber and soon had everything in working order again. The snow was dry, making the task all the easier. Again I was glad for this characteristic Far Northern dryness which, when you're trying to mold a snowman, means you have to use water. I reloaded the magazine, just in case. Then we started for the bull moose, a still dark heap a hundred feet upstream.

At first, I mostly held while Brad butchered the animal with the neat help of a small meat saw from Bushman's pack, laying the muzzle, tongue, heart, liver and kidneys carefully to one side, as they are the tastiest parts of the animal. Then, using my own small sheath knife that a Florida friend, W. D. Randall, Jr., had made by hand especially for me, I helped with the skinning. We had to get the moose cut up and ready to pack home before it froze.

When you're trying to manipulate an animal as heavy as a horse, that can get to be a lot of bulk to move around. But the flesh was gratifyingly warm against my chilled fingers. Until we could bring Chinook and Cloud up the north shore, there wasn't much we could do with the chunks down in the river canyon but pile them in a well-ventilated heap, then drape the hollow-haired hide loosely over them in case of more snow.

By that time, I had a driftwood fire crackling, tea brewing and several strips of dark-red liver broiling on a green-stick rack.

It was close to the cliff and Brad sat with me on a cleared, bough-softened rock between the fire and a ledge, where the warmth could reflect on our backs, the first thing outdoorsmen from hotter climes learn to do in subzero weather.

Snow had started to slant earthward again in great, chalky streaks, as Bushman joined us in savoring the rich meat. Night was fast lifting over the land. *Lift* was the word, too. Night does not fall. I saw darkness rising, filling Rocky Mountain Canyon with deepening gloom. The high peaks behind us, between which avalanche-packed Starfish Creek cut its solitary channel, were still bright with sunlight.

But the sun sank lower and lower behind the towering mound of Bullhead as a vagrant night breeze, the last remnant of the recent tumultuous wind, whispered down the chasm. Long shafts of yellow light sought the ravines of this great peak, through which the river had cut after moraine had clogged its original channel. The portage road now passed over that site. Deepening azure shadows clotted in pools on the burned, bare incline on the other side of the ice.

"It's going to be a dark night and a slippery one," Brad said, slim fingers clasped around his long legs. "Are you sure you want to walk five miles and take the chance, at the end, of getting a tree branch in the eye? We've everything we need for the night right here, shelter a few hundred yards down the shore, and all the meat we can eat."

"What about the horses?" I said doubtfully.

"I threw them an extra bundle apiece this morning, just in case. The snow will continue to give them all the water they need. Besides, Vena, we haven't bivouacked for too long."

"If it won't be too much work for you. . . ."

"Nothing to it," he promised. "We'll just take the tenderloins for ourselves tonight, a bit of liver for breakfast, some ribs for Bushman, then move down to where the woods border the river just above Box Canyon."

I remembered how much I'd always liked the primitiveness of building what Brad referred to as an Indian camp. One was quickly and easily fashioned. Too, it would be cozy and comfortable with a long fire in front. When properly erected, it would withstand a heavy storm. The gray night closed in on the earth, as more and more snowflakes drifted down through the heavy, cold air. The trees, bare except for the conifers, were silent and brooding along the shore.

Using a booted foot, Brad quickly made a clearing for the fire on a flat stretch of north shore. A single match started flames sputtering through a tight handful of the dead, little, resin-filled twigs you find underneath all evergreens. Brad wigwamed dry wood from a standing dead poplar above this.

"There you are, honey," he said.

I piled a great heap of dead branches atop this blazing nucleus for better visibility, then set forth with my knife to cut a quantity of long, thickly needled spruce limbs for our lean-to. These I carried to where we were going to sleep, first piling them loosely around a long upside-down poplar limb with an upwardly slanting branch at its end—then lifting them in a bulky, but surprisingly light, bundle.

Tall, slim poplar saplings thrust themselves skyward where we were working. Five minutes sufficed for Brad to drop one of them, cut a seven-foot pole from it, lay one end in a tree crotch handy to the fire and tie the other end at the same height to a big lodgepole pine, using a leather lace from the dog pack.

"Well, there's our ridgepole," he said in passing.

So that we'd get maximum direct and reflected warmth from the fire, he'd placed this ridge just high enough for us to sit comfortably upright beneath it. Now he followed through by slanting most of my long spruce boughs from the ridgepole to the ground, in an angle just wide enough to accommodate the two of us sleeping side by side lengthwise to the fire. He laced the remaining limbs across these horizontally for additional thickness. Then he cut down several young spruce and leaned them at the two triangular ends of the structure, closing it in except at the mouth.

"Now for the bed," he said.

Together we gathered armfuls of the springiest, bushiest spruce boughs we could find, then thatched a browse bed a foot thick. It was soft and inviting. Bushman appropriated one end of it with the bones he was gnawing.

"That looks good," Brad said, pausing in his task of hauling in enough dry wood to last the night. The Big Dipper hung as brightly as a lantern-lit signpost in the blue-black sky. "Say, aren't you hungry all over again, too? What say we have a few kabobs before turning in? If you'll char them a bit, we won't notice the lack of salt. Give me the tea pail and I'll fill it with ice for you."

While he was gone, I angled a long green pole between two stones to hold the pail. Then I cut walnut-sized chunks of meat from one of the tenderloins and threaded them on two sharpened green willow wands, alternating each with a small wild onion from a patch Brad had found deep in the windswept sand on the shore.

The identifying slender, quill-like leaves had shriveled, but the one and only characteristic on which to depend, *the onion odor*, was there. Wild onions—including leeks, chives and garlics— grow all over North America except in the farthest northern regions. Indians have always sought them to enliven their meals. The milder of them are delicious raw. Incidentally, you should have nothing whatsoever to do with any plants, wild or otherwise, that resemble the onion but do not have its familiar odor! Some bulbs whose appearance is superficially like that of onions are among our most concentrated poisons. Your nose will be your own best protector. If there's any doubt, do without.

I held the two sagging wands over a portion of our campfire where poplar had crumbled to cherry-red coals, then Brad came and relieved me of his. The kabobs, black outside but juicily pink within, were still sizzling when we bit them gingerly off the sticks. Never had meat been more tender and succulent, nor

Looking upriver from in front of the present cabin. The Peace cuts through the backbone of the Canadian Rockies.

Rocky Mountain Canyon, just a few feet below where the Peace River is now dammed.

The still frozen beaver pond opposite the cabin.

A favorite style of dovetailed corner, with the traditional ground-hugging lowness of log construction emphasized by Bushman.

onions more delectable, washed down as they were with cup after cup of steaming black tea in our stainless-steel cups from Abercrombie & Fitch, as cool to the lips as crockery.

"I thought meat had to be aged to be so good," I told Brad with some surprise.

"It's a funny thing," he said, "but it's just as delicious fresh as when it's been aged properly for a week or ten days."

"Well, that explodes another theory."

The thin snow, now driving more assertively from the east and lodging on my jacket and hair, consisted of beautiful star crystals, not chubby and cottony but substantial and partly transparent. They were about a tenth of an inch thick, perfect little tireless wheels with six spokes or, rather, six perfect tiny leaflets, fern-like, with distinct straight and slender midribs raying from the center. As Thoreau had noted:

> *How full of creative genius is the air in which they are generated. I should hardly admire more if real stars fell and lodged on my coat.*
>
> *We are snowed on with gems. What a world we live in! Where are the jewelers' shops? There is nothing handsomer than a snow-flake. I may say that the maker of the world exhausts his skill with each snowflake and dewdrop he sends down. We think that one mechanically coheres and that the other simply flows together and falls, but in truth they are the product of enthusiasm, the children of an ecstasy, finished with the artist's utmost skill.*

Before we turned in, Brad scraped the snow into little mounds against the three sides of our lean-to to shut out ground drafts. Then he built up the blaze, which was extended the length of the shelter, until we fairly basked in warmth.

"We'll have to stoke the fire every two or three hours all night," he said, "but if you won't mind my reaching over you, you can sleep on the outside next to it. You'll be coziest that way."

"But will you be warm enough?"

"Feel for yourself," he said. "The slant of this lean-to is just right; the back wall is reflecting the heat on me perfectly."

"We'll take turns feeding the fire," I decreed. "Whoever wakes up first can do it."

"All right," he said. "Whoever it is will fall right back to sleep, anyway."

A pair of whisper-winged owls, hunting, exchanged their whoo-whoo-whooing in the cold, snow-scoured darkness. In the distance a lone wolf howled, then howled again, without getting an answer. Far above, I could hear the wind surging up the canyon. When I asked him to listen, Brad could hear it, too, as if we were loosening our ties with the earth to attend to the Homeric music of sirens.

"There is always a kind of fine aeolian-harp music to be heard in the air," Thoreau asserted. "I hear now, as it were, the mellow sound of distant horns in the hollow mansions of the upper air, a sound to make all men divinely insane that hear it, far away overhead, subsiding into my ear. To ears that are expanded what a harp this world is!"

That outdoor night on the aromatic spruce mattress, with live heat from the lifting fire beating upon us, was one of the snuggest I have ever spent, although we learned later from Dudley that the temperature had plummeted far below zero. When I awoke for the last time in the grayness of dawn, Brad already had tea brewing and two long slabs of liver ready to go on forked green sticks over a bed of hardwood coals he had raked to one edge of the roaring blaze.

"These should only cook two minutes a side," he said, "so do you want to get ready to eat?"

Well browned outside but still red and juicy within, the fresh moose liver was tasty even without salt. There are some, of course, who prefer their liver done somewhat more than this; every gourmet to his own taste. Too much overcooking, however, gives you a leathery, tasteless and far less nutritious dish.

The sun rose downriver that morning while we were on our way home, half of it lying on the rim of the horizon for long minutes—bloated, swollen and enormous, magnified as it was by the earth's atmosphere. It was almost entirely decorative at this time of day, creating only a pale, warmless gleam in the whitened wilderness. Behind us it brought alive the silent, glittering, soaring furrows of Bullhead Mountain, silhouetted like a tremendous, poised comber against the azure sky.

It was bitterly cold away from the surging cheerfulness of the fire; my joints felt creaky and my fingers numb. I must have walked half an hour before warmth began to seep into my toes. Then a snow-laced wind came up to swath the lodgepole pines on the flats above us in drifting whiteness. I kept feeling my face for any numb spots and when an ear began to feel wooden beneath my exploring fingers, I cupped a bared warm palm over it. The old-fashioned supposition that a frostbitten part should be rubbed with snow has long ago been disproved.

"It's getting colder," Brad said. "Hear those trees crack."

I felt as if I were cold within rather than without, for I was not shivering. My very soul seemed to be freezing and my brain shriveling to the dimensions of a highbush cranberry. I kept putting one foot ahead of the other and continued feeling my face to make sure that no part of it became stiff, all the while watching Brad for any signs of white patches. The tip of my nose was the next place to lose feeling, but my cupped warm palm soon had it tingling again. It was as if the river channel were a trough filled with liquid air and I felt that if I could just climb out of it, I would warm up again. Then there was the great slanting ledge and, following our well-trodden trail up the slope toward the cabin, I stepped back into reality once more.

The horses were whinnying and Brad threw them bundles, holding each with the blade of his knife against the twine so that as he tossed it the binding was cut, loosening the stalks of golden oats. Chinook and Cloud immediately buried their icicled noses in the grain. Bushman squirmed into the cabin ahead of us.

"Home!" I enthused.

"Uuuummm," Brad echoed.

We had left fuzzsticks and kindling all ready for the big iron cookstove and the airtight heater. Brad, ducking his head beneath the doorway to the second room, busied himself with the heater while I scattered the accumulation of ashes through the grate of the cookstove with the lid lifter. Then I laid in the necessary little heap of fuzzsticks, but my ungloved fingers proved to be too numb to hold the long wooden match. I was trying for the third time when Brad, striding back into the main room, took over. Soon firelight was glinting in his frost-rimmed blue eyes and from where I stood I could see that he was smiling. Wonderful, popping, crackling warmth began dancing about me.

"Why don't you stay here and unpack Bush?" Brad said, picking up two buckets and an ax. "I'll go down to the river for water."

I held my hands over the stove until my fingers would flex again, then assaulted the frozen knot at the top of the wolfhound's pack until it came loose. Inside were the remains of the liver and tenderloins, the tongue, heart, fat-sheathed kidneys and the muzzle. I took out the last of these, leaving the rest where they were for Brad to transfer to the cold cache when he had climbed back with the slopping pails. It was the kind of day for cooking moose muzzle.

"The greatest delicacies of the North American wilderness," Vilhjalmur Stefansson, most eminent of this century's terrestrial explorers, had just written Brad, "are moose muzzle, beaver tail, buffalo hump, caribou brisket, and ling liver; all of them the delicious fat that it is now the fashion to condemn."

We'd enjoyed them all here in Hudson Hope, the bison from a delectably orange-streaked chunk Ted Boynton had brought back from a hunting trip. He'd cooked for the expedition downriver near Great Slave Lake. But if there was any best in my estimation, it was what I was holding now.

When I first heard the term moose muzzle, I'd thought of the ruff of erectile hair on the huge ruminant's neck. It was Brad who set me straight. Moose muzzle is merely another name for moose nose. Brad had cut off this unlikely section yesterday by sawing off the large upper jaw just below the eyes. I knew enough now not to try to skin it.

Instead, I scalded it in a pot of bubbling water for about an hour, then cooled it and plucked out the thick hair. Afterward, lounging in the heavenly warmth of the open oven with a first edition of Jeffrey Farnol's *The Amateur Gentleman*, I cooked it to a point just short of boiling in fresh water. Along with salt and pepper and several whole onions, I cooked it until the white meat fell away from the nostrils and dark strips loosened from the bones and jowls. In the meantime, the Dutch oven I was using sent forth tantalizing clouds of pure wilderness splendor, presaging a warm, sweet, fragrant feast.

Moose muzzle cooked this way is fine to pick at hot, as we proved that noon. I had grilled tenderloin steaks, too, so enough of the nose was left to allow the juices and meat to jell together, to be savored later in cold slices.

"The meat will be all right up there for another day, won't it?" I asked Brad. "I don't feel much like packing it in this afternoon."

"Sure," he said. "Tomorrow will be fine. Where did you put Farnol's *The Broad Highway*? I'd like to read that again. I'd better clean our rifles first, though."

We decided not to take our guns the next day. We did not intend to do any hunting and they would only be something else to carry.

Brad wasn't even riding, putting a crosstree pack saddle on Chinook and leading her instead. I rode a McClellan saddle upriver, as that could be easily packed, but I would be leading Cloud back. The weather had warmed again; a brisk wind was blowing downriver once more instead of from the stormy northeast. We followed Dudley's trapping trail past our former homesite on the north flat. Leaving the sheltering trees at the point where we had built the lean-to, then picking our way, I led Cloud along the rocks and ledges of the north shore.

We were just ambling along; I was idly wondering if we could work my adventure into an article for one of the big outdoor magazines, when ahead of us Bushman came to an abrupt halt. He was growling low in his throat. As we started to round the wooded point just below where the meat was heaped, he began barking ferociously.

The brown, humped shape of a bear was sniffing at the pile of moose meat. Grizzly! Bushman was nearer me and I hurried the few necessary steps forward to grab his collar. At my abrupt movement in its direction, the grizzly reared up on its hind legs. It looked at least ten feet tall and its broad head was swaying from one side to the other, incongruously small eyes glaring at us.

There was nowhere on the river for us to go. Even if there had been a nearby tree which we could have climbed, I don't think I could have left Bushman to face the danger alone, especially not after he had saved my life two days before. Now I remembered what a knot of old sourdoughs, lounging about the stove in the post office, had said one time when we'd gone in together for the mail.

Brad must have recalled it at the same instant, for now he said in a low voice, "Don't move. Keep Bushman quiet."

"If you're ever confronted in the open with an unharmed wild animal and you're not about to shoot it," Bill Carter had said, "stand still and begin talking as calmly as you can manage."

Ted Boynton had nodded. "That's right. For cripe's sake—excuse me, Vena—don't start running. That's an invitation for the animal to chase you. Just like a dog attacking a moving car. When the auto's parked you don't see him charging it."

Moving slowly so as not to startle the grizzly again, I held Bushman's jaws closed with my free hand. He whined and struggled briefly, then remained alertly quiet.

"Hungry, are you, Old Eph?" I heard Brad saying in as conversational a tone as he could manage. "Well, that's our meat. We need it to stay alive. You go and get some meat of your own. Let's be peaceable about it, though."

The grizzly's head stilled. Brad kept on talking, just saying anything; what I've recounted is all I can remember of the one-sided conversation. Then, as if satisfied by its scrutiny that these strangers were offering no immediate danger, the bear dropped back to all fours, turning with the motion, and shuffled away up-river. Scarcely daring to breathe, I watched its brown bulk disappearing around a corner in the direction of Bullhead.

"Whew," Brad said then. "Let me hold Cloud while you put Bushman on a leash. We don't want any more encounters."

The two horses were skittish and Brad had to rub their noses with moose blood before, pulling the hide to one side, he could get them close enough to load.

"We're lucky, Vena," he said. "It must have been that grizzly whose trail we crossed the other day. It apparently only smelled the meat. If it'd actually started eating it, I doubt if it would have been so willing to leave."

"Let's get away from here," I said.

"All right with me," he said. "Tie Bushman to a rock. Then if you'll help me steady this hind quarter on the crosstree, I'll get the other one up and rope them in place. Then I can pile the ribs between and diamond hitch the pack cover over everything. We can put the fore quarters and the rest on Cloud."

Soon the horses were packed and we were on the homeward trail. As sometimes happens, that moose had come hard all the way. Sky, mountains and river quieted into deeper shades of blue as we walked back toward the cabin. The air stilled, serenely and harmoniously, as if to mull over all that had occurred. Again the day, the past, was blending with the future night.

8

Wolf Pack

At length, winter started in earnest and the hunting season ended before we secured our second so-necessary moose. Just as I finished chinking the log walls, luckily on a warm chinooking day, the seasonal winds began to howl around the cabin as if they had not had permission to do so till then.

Brad, working inside on bad days, had transformed the main room into an acme of tidy compactness. Our large double bunk, beneath which duffle bags and firewood were stored, occupied the northwest corner. Upon this wooden shelf our softly inflated air mattresses, covered by roomy individual goose-down sleeping bags, adjusted themselves to every changing tangent of our bodies, more comfortably than the finest city bed on which I had ever slept.

The great iron cookstove was within reach of Brad, who slept on the outside. He got into the habit of letting the fire die out directly after dinner each evening so that he could lay the makings for the next day's blaze before retiring. These consisted of three or four carefully arranged fuzzsticks, atop which were spread thinly cut dry spruce kindling that would begin snapping and popping once he dropped in a lighted match.

Brad always had a number of fuzzsticks prepared in advance, selecting the straightest grained kindling for them and fashioning each by whittling shaving after shaving, not detaching any, until the stick became a fan of curling, resin-filled strips of softwood, ready to flare into life at the touch of a match. He kept regular firewood in a handy pile, ready to shove into the stove once the fire was chortling merrily. He prepared a saucepan of cereal the night before, so that all he had to do in the early morning was slide it over the hottest lid.

His favorite forenoon meal was oatmeal and we found that the quickly cooking variety saved time. He added one-half cup of oatmeal and one-half teaspoon of salt to two cups of cold water. A quarter cup of seedless raisins, more or less, plumped out during the night to add flavor. The next morning he hunched far enough out of his sleeping bag to get things going, letting the pot come to a boil before easing it to one side for a few minutes. Then he added a liberal spoonful of margarine, which spread in a rich golden flood. This was really luxury. Deepening cold had condensed and some twenty feet above the throbbing earth was a twinkling ceiling of ice crystals through which the smoke of our solitary fire ascended in an unwavering pillar. He could just as easily have made enough extra oatmeal for me, of course, but I preferred to drowse a half hour longer.

On the other side of the stove, in the cabin's northeast corner, was my tiny kitchen: a three-sided counter with shelves for food and utensils underneath, as well as room to set the water buckets. Warm water came from a well at the back of the stove and from the titanic steaming teakettle. Above were more shelves and cabinets for food and dishes.

A couch, on which I used to lounge and read, stretched beneath the long eastern window on that side of the log wall. It was wedged tightly between the kitchen cabinet at its foot and Brad's shelves for books, manuscripts, paper and other writing supplies at the top, giving me solid backing against which to lean my kapok pillows.

Brad's office occupied the southeast corner, fronted on the south by the dining room table which he cleared every day after work so that we could use it for eating. Then there was another large easy chair, this one for me, the door to the outside, then in the northwest corner—extending as far along the west wall as the door to the second room, on the other side of which started the bunk—a large double closet, across which I hung a black-and-white checkered cloth to keep out the dust.

There was also room to scatter several upright chairs, some of which we kept around a handy bridge table in the center of the room. When there was company, it supplemented the fully opened dining room table so that we could accommodate six banqueters.

"Aw-wa-oooo-ooh." The howl of a nearby timber wolf, spine-tingling in the February darkness, sounded from a dry canyon directly across the Peace River. I'd been hearing wolves for the past few years, but their wild voices still made the back of my neck tingle. A wolf sounds different when you and your husband are the sole humans within miles. "Aw-wa-oooooo."

The silver sickle of the February moon hung over the cabin, higher than the evening star that dangled beneath it like a pendant on a platinum loop. The fire in the big cookstove beside the bunk had been long out; I could tell by the feel of the cabin that only a few embers, if any, remained of what had been a roaring blaze in the airtight heater in the adjacent room. My pneumatic mattress, cushioning every changing angle of my body, was soft beneath me. The wolf sounded hungry.

Then the whole pack joined in. It was like two express trains going in opposite directions at a grade crossing, whistles wide open. The wolves must have killed something, I thought. There were a lot of moose now in the beaver meadows across river. They must have brought down a moose. Chinooks had necessitated my canning much of our first moose and we needed fresh meat, too.

The week before we'd found the newly stripped skeleton of a moose upriver and brought back some of the marrow bones. Dog-like tracks had been so thick around the remaining bones and hair that they had almost made a skating rink in the snow, so I knew how ravenously timber wolves ate. In a very short time there wouldn't be much left of that moose across river. Then I saw Brad was getting up and starting to dress.

"What are you doing?" I asked drowsily. "It isn't morning yet, is it? Quiet, Bushman."

"Hear those wolves?" he asked. "They've got a moose right across river. We're not likely to get one any closer."

"What do you mean, *we*?" I asked. "The wolves have it."

"I'm going to take it from the wolves."

"You can't!" I was horrified at the idea. "You mustn't. They'd never give it up without a fight, and it's night, and you can't see to shoot."

"I won't have to shoot anything," he said; there was enough moonlight for me to see him reaching for his fleecy red shirt.

"But they've had a taste of it. You said that you probably couldn't have talked that grizzly away from our meat if he'd already started eating it."

"Wolves aren't grizzlies. They won't put up any argument." He lit the coal oil lamp and started rummaging around the shelves behind his office chair. "Where are our new flashlight batteries, Vena?"

"We haven't any. You used the last of them getting home in that storm two evenings ago."

"That's right. I'll have to make a torch." He sat down and started to pull on the heavy woolen gray-and-red socks I had knitted him for Christmas. "What are you doing, getting up, too? There's nothing you can do, Vena, not until daylight."

"Daylight," I said, swinging my feet to the cold floor. "That's it. Why don't you wait for daylight, at least?"

"Because the best part of the meat will be all gone by then," he said reasonably. "I mean, we'll have to wait until daylight before you can help me start bringing it back to our cache. You get back in bed now."

I could hear my voice answering him; it was as if I were two people.

"You're not going over there all alone, Brad."

"But there's not the slightest danger," he insisted, stopping and looking full at me. "The wolves will just dissolve into the landscape when they hear and smell a human being."

"I'm not going to stay here and let you go over there all by yourself," I said desperately. "If there's really no danger, all the better. But I couldn't bear staying here by myself."

"You'd have Bushman," he told me.

"You're not going to take Bush?" I asked.

"A dog is a different proposition," Brad explained. "The wolves would lure him off into the bush and gang up on him. Hurry up if you're coming. I'll go out and get the torch ready."

"You're not starting without me?" I said anxiously.

"I won't be any further away than the woodpile," he promised. "Stay, Bushman."

It didn't take me long to get ready. By the time I'd pulled on my rubber-bottomed L.L. Bean leather boots, Brad reappeared with a strip of birch bark a foot wide and about three feet long. He folded this into thicknesses lengthwise, making a three-ply strip about four inches by three feet. Then he split one end of a four-foot green pole he was carrying. The split of the pole held the bark strip about eight inches from one end.

"Is that all you're going to need?" I asked.

"It'll last for fifteen to twenty minutes," he said. "We won't light it until we're on the other side of the river. In the meantime, there's enough moonlight to see by."

The wolves were howling again when we left the cabin. I don't know if that was why I was shivering or whether it was because of the chill of the northern winter night. Anyway, the thing I had to do was stay close to Brad and keep my wits about me. Safe or not, I was glad he'd brought his rifle.

We started down the slope to the river sidewise, newly fallen snow building about our feet. The frozen Peace glowed whitely ahead of us, as though illuminated by a ghostly inner incandescence. Then I felt its hardness beneath my soles.

When we reached the timbered steepness of the other side, Brad applied a flaming wooden kitchen match to the torch. The birch bark sputtered redly, with a sweet black smoke. Brad held the short, burning end downward for a moment so that the fire could climb. The light revealed all the ground, bushes and trees within about twenty feet.

When I climbed the bank where a frozen brook ribboned over huge boulders, I was really breathing hard. The sun didn't hit much on this side. The snow was nearly two feet deep and it was crusted from chinooks. I didn't suppose the noise would make any difference, though. We weren't trying to stalk anything.

The wolf chorus pierced the living darkness again, so deafening that it seemed to be sounding from every direction. It gave me some second thoughts, I can tell you. Timber wolves at Hudson Hope grew to weigh 180 pounds. I realized that they are normally so cautious that a human seldom sees one but, for all I knew, driving them away from a fresh kill might be something else again. But Brad and I were already close to them and I wasn't going to turn back now.

I knew from previous explorations that this side of Rocky Mountain Canyon was broken up by old river channels of past centuries. The bottoms of these had become muskegs; peat bogs in the making. Now that the morasses were frozen beneath the snow, we could walk on them without sinking.

Brad kept bearing upriver. As the bark burned, he shoved more of it through the split in the stick handle. It gave an eerie, shadowridden light. Ahead of me, upwind, I heard a loud snap as if a thigh bone had been broken by a savage jaw. That started me shaking again, only this time I knew it wasn't from cold.

"Vena Angier," I told myself resolutely, "you're going to feel a lot better when some of that moose meat is in your stomach."

All the time, though, I was hoping that it wouldn't be us in the wolves' stomachs.

Except for the stir of wind among pine needles, it was quiet all of a sudden. When we rounded the next dark corner, there was the black bulk of the moose sprawled on the snow. A couple of big gray animals were zigzagging away, just like shifty football halfbacks. I thought for an instant that I'd been mistaken and that they were large sled dogs. Then I saw the way their eyes slanted, reflecting firelight. The next instant they disappeared into the shadows.

"Boy, oh boy, oh boy," Brad was saying. Wolves must have been still skulking in the bushes, but they weren't showing themselves or making any noise. I felt extremely weak, but he was talking casually. "Wasn't that something, honey?"

I raised my face and kissed him. Then he unslung his rifle, set it aside and stuck the torch in the snow. He smoothed both of his gloved hands along my cheeks and kissed me on the mouth. His fingers shifted very gradually, very softly over my hair and neck. I felt the leanness of his body tight against me and his arms around mine, which were at my sides; then I wriggled them loose and returned his pressure, tautly and tenderly and savagely.

"I love you," he said.

"I love you, too," I whispered back, although I hadn't meant it to be a whisper: my throat felt tight, constricted.

"Well," he said finally, "we'd better get a fire going."

There was still enough left of the torch to light the little mound of resinous dead twigs and branches we piled together. The dry evergreen heaped atop this crackling nucleus was soon snapping and sparking. I found a half-fallen dead poplar sapling that I broke into sections with my feet so that we would have some hardwood coals to hold the campfire.

Not much was left of the underneath of that moose—a dry cow, from the looks of her thick fat—but bones and long blackish hair. The wolves hadn't reached the back steaks, though, and these were our favorites. Too, most of the quarters were intact. Interestingly, Brad showed me, they hadn't hamstrung this moose, as I'd read wolves did, but had attacked her throat.

"Will we have to start packing the meat home now," I asked, "before the wolves come back?"

"They won't be back," Brad said. "We may as well start skinning it out now, though, before it begins to freeze. You can build that fire up higher if you want, so that we can see better; I'll get started."

"How will we get it over to the cache?" I wondered aloud.

"It's just across the river and even though the horses aren't shod, they shouldn't slip if we take our time, especially with the snow. We'll wait for daylight before we start packing, though. Right now, what do you want to bring home for breakfast?"

"Matt and Erna Boe had some fresh eggs the last time I was in town and I got a dozen," I told him. "What would you say to kidneys and scrambled eggs?"

"Fine," Brad agreed. "And we'll take back one of these shins for Bushman, as soon as I can disjoint it."

I thought of King Gething that dawn as I prepared our breakfast.

"If I could eat just once more, I'd sure pick me bear kidneys," King had told us once at his lone coal mine, high on the eastern slope of Bullhead Mountain. "I'd want 'em simmered awhile with butter, salt, cloves, celery if I had any, and a mite of onion. Matter of fact, let's get 'em on the fire before someone else shows up."

That had established my recipe for big game kidneys. You start by dividing the kidneys into segments about the size of chicken hearts. All you have to do with bear kidneys to achieve this is to strip away the connective membrane. Moose kidneys are solid, though, and you must cut them up.

I simmer the meat over low heat, with the other ingredients, until it's tender. The best way to establish proportions, I've found, is by taste. The tidbits, along with the eggs, were especially tasty that morning atop hot crusty bannock, steaming with margarine. A cloud sailed serenely over the dawn-quickened horizon as we ate, trailing its chill blue shadows across the picture window.

It took us most of the morning to get the meat hanging in our cache. Bushman, whom we kept safely on a leash, helped with a pack load of the more delicate parts, but there was no further sign of the wolf pack. We took everything edible, even the brains this time. With their outer membrane removed, dipped in beaten egg, rolled in cracker or bannock crumbs, seasoned to taste with salt and black pepper, then sauteed uncovered in margarine, these have a delicate flavor that goes well with scrambled eggs.

"Nothing is going to waste in this household," I vowed.

The tongue was another delicacy we didn't allow to get by us. Those from the larger ruminants are especial tidbits, that from an adult moose being as large as a beef tongue. In case you've heretofore passed up this choice bit, there's a trick to securing it. Feel for the bones under the lower jaw. Make a deep slit lengthwise between them, up into the mouth. Press the tongue down through this opening. Grasp it and cut it off as close to the base as possible.

Cover with cold, salted water and bring to a boil. Spoon off any scum that floats to the surface. Then simmer until the meat is fork tender. When it has cooled sufficiently in the stock to permit its being handled easily, skin it. A sharp knife will help, although much of the tough skin can be peeled off by the fingers alone. Remove any small bones at the base.

Moose, deer, caribou and elk tongue is particularly good thinly sliced, either hot or cold. If you want something special, smoke the cooked and peeled tongue over a smudge of ground birch, alder, willow or similar hardwood for several hours.

With fifty-pound sacks of Bushman's dog meal hanging from horizontal wires where the Disneylike little wood mice couldn't reach them and a few wild vegetables—such as bunches of little pearly onions—also suspended out of harm's way, the overhead part of the cache was now full. In the storage room off the main part of the cabin, where it wouldn't hurt if the fire went out, were cans of dried vegetables, large cartons of dried fruits, including the best available apples and peaches and apricots, a metal barrel in which we kept our flour and sugar, and shelves of jams, jellies, dried milk, dried eggs, and various odds and ends.

The jars of canned wild meat and juicy wild fruits—raspberries, saskatoons and luscious strawberries—which freezing would crack, we kept safely with the bags of potatoes and other garden vegetables in the shelved cold cellar. It had been dug below the frost level, reached by a trapdoor in the main cabin floor.

It was a cozy feeling, having everything we might need for months to come securely about us. That evening, removing a lid of the cookstove and stretching a steel grill across the opening to broil back steaks, I looked outside just in time to see an owl sweep by: a mute, moving darkness against the moon. In the distance a lone wolf howled. I stirred the glowing bed of hardwood coals with more pleasure than usual.

9

How Can You Stand the Cold?

"But how can you stand the cold, dark winters?" ask many of those who write to us at Hudson Hope. Incidentally, we answer each and every letter of the average seven or eight that now arrive daily at this Canadian post office and which our friend, Postmaster Noreen Stubley, as she prefers to be called, forwards to us if we happen to be away on a trip. But getting back to "stand the cold" . . .

It's really a matter of semantics. We don't actually *stand* the winters: we *revel* in them. After the rousing springs and the bracing autumns, they are our favorite season. No time of the year is more dramatic, more stimulating; in the wonderful seclusion they afford us and the time to concentrate on writing, they are the best of all.

In fact, the season we like least is the hot, enervating, insect-ridden, pilgrim-thronged summer. All in all, summer in the wilderness is a pretty good season at that, but it's not up to our far northern winters.

Our outdoor employment now was collecting the dead wood in the forest and bringing it to the cabin: in our hands, on our shoulders, but mostly—now that snow was here to make the job easier—by tying a log with two half hitches to the tail of one or another of our saddle horses. This we did by looping the first hitch on the extended tail and then the other on the tail after the hair has been bent back upon itself. Cloud and Chinook, thus impeded at the center of their gravities, really laid into the work and soon skidded the timber beside Brad's sawhorses in front of the cabin. Here he sliced it into stove-sized portions with his thin-bladed Swede saw, then split it on the chopping block, ready for me to stack.

An old split rail fence of Dudley's, which had seen its best days, was a great haul for us. Like Thoreau, we "sacrificed it to Vulcan, for it was past serving the god Terminus. How much more interesting an event is that man's supper who had just been forth in the snow to hunt the fuel to cook it with."

A few pieces of fat pine were a great treasure. It is interesting to remember how much of this food for fire is still concealed in the bowels of the earth. Brad and I often spent a sunny afternoon prospecting for such fuel over a chinook-bared hillside behind the cabin, where a pitch pine woods had formerly stood and we could dig out the fat pine roots.

These are almost indestructible. Stumps thirty to forty years old were still sound at the core, although the sapwood had nearly all become vegetable mold within the scale of thick bark that formed a ring, level with the earth, four or five inches distant from the heart. With old ax and shovel, we explored these mines and followed the marrowy store, yellow as a vein of gold, deep into the earth. This was unexcelled for starting the fire in the bedside cookstove mornings as, while the handful of villagers beyond the forested horizon were lighting their own blazes, a smoky stream from our chimney gave notice to the wild inhabitants of Rocky Mountain Canyon that Brad, at least, was awake.

Freshly cut green birch, although we liked the trees so much that we felled but few of them, answered my cooking needs better than anything else. I often left a green birch fire in the cookstove when we left to take a stroll on a winter afternoon; when we returned, three or four hours afterward, it would still be alive and glowing, as if I had left a cheerful and trustworthy house-keeper behind. But our cabin occupied so sheltered a position and was so small and well chinked, that with our snug sleeping bags we could afford to let both fires go out most nights.

Some of my city friends spoke in their letters as though I had come to the north woods purposely to freeze myself. The animal merely makes a bed, which he warms with his body, in a sheltered place. But man, having discovered fire, boxes up some air in a spacious apartment and warms that, making it his bed in which he can move about divested of most cumbersome clothing; thus maintaining a kind of summer in the midst of winter.

But the most luxuriously housed man has little to boast of in this respect, Thoreau believed, nor need we trouble ourselves to speculate how the human race might be at last totally destroyed. It would be easy to cut our threads at any time with a little sharper blast from the north. We go on dating from Cold Fridays and Great Snows, but a little colder Friday or greater snow would put a period to man's existence on the globe.

This would be especially true, I thought now, in cities where people are so dependent on fuel gathered by others in different parts of the world. Here in the woods, at least, our means of keeping ourselves snug was as close as the forest. Here, too, our firewood warmed us twice: first when we were getting it in, then again in the stove; no fuel could give forth more heat.

The sun sank early these winter days, not appearing in the south-southeast until after ten o'clock in the morning, then disappearing in the south-southwest, usually in an awe-inspiring sunset, shortly after two o'clock in the afternoon. It never extended very high above the horizon—which in our case was the wooded ridge that formed the southern edge of the prehistoric river channels—but lingered just below the level of visibility for well over an hour at each end of daylight. Brad, who disliked working by lamplight, got into the habit of writing all the sunlit hours by our four-sashed south window. Then he did his outside chores between the time that the eternal clock disappeared and the dark still night finally rose and blotted out the world.

Likely as not, I was occupied during this active period with my own typewriter at my end of the table; with brushes, oils and canvas; with making flour and sourdough starter spell bread; or outdoors with my birch-withe broom, sweeping dry snow out of the paths.

Here, in this dry cold, it was possible to appreciate the six-pointed intricacies of each flake. No two of the billions and billions of them were ever exactly alike. The snow-catching, and therefore visible, wind curled back upon itself at trees and bushes, creating little drifts behind each protuberance, be it no more than a brown blade of grass.

I tried making snowmen, but for one of these I had to build a campfire and melt water. Our northern snowflakes were far too dry to cling together with the sodden lack of individuality seen in the slushy cities. The two horses regarded the storms stoically, although these made leading them to water in the winter unnecessary, for they ate snow with great relish. Bushman found it intriguing stuff in which to frolic, leaping some drifts and thrusting himself stiff-legged through others. He was a tall dog; standing with his forefeet braced against Brad's shoulders, he could reach a chunk of meat held as high as my husband could reach.

But there was seldom much snow during a Hudson Hope winter, this being a semiarid portion of the continent. Never was it so deep that we could not ride our horses where we would. Nor, on foot, did we ever have to resort to the snowshoes we had brought. During the midst of winter we found it easiest to travel the river, where overflow from the constantly moving stream cleared the way along the edges, then refroze into a smooth sidewalk.

It is the intervals of extreme cold that are most spectacular. One of them occurred while I was writing this. The sun had just vanished, touching the ridge above Starfish Creek and shattering into a thousand fragments of crimson fire. The deep blue shadows which had been crawling up the inclines now overpowered them and sped up into the lower heavens, where the evening star burned like a little platinum flame. I realized it had suddenly grown much colder, as behind me Brad shouldered open the door, arms piled high with firewood to store beneath the double bunk.

I left my typewriter, too, and went outside to fill the Coleman pressure lantern from a red gasoline can. I'd gone outdoors in just an extra sweater, but when I came in with the lantern, after pumping it with air, I zippered on my scarlet goose-down jacket before venturing forth again. I checked the thermometer on the porch post, a few yards from the picture window, just from curiosity. It was only six degrees below zero, but there was a chill in the nipping wind that had started to seep into the wilderness from the northeast.

"Want to get the water now?" I asked Brad.

"You bet," he said; I went back inside to get the three buckets, while he moved toward the woodpile for the ax.

He took a pair of buckets and the ax in one mittened hand and preceded me gingerly down the icy trail, exceptionally slippery because snow had been squalling now and then during the day. That fall we had cut steps in the clay; that made the descent easier, particularly as Brad had strung tan hemp lines among the birch trees beside the path. Sure enough, despite its spruce-bough covering, the water hole had skimmed over and it took several hearty raps with the ax to reopen it enough to wield the dipper to fill the pails.

"Brrrr. I'd hate to go through the ice on a day like this," Brad said.

"So would I. Here's hoping we never do."

Bushman, who'd romped down to the ledge, preceded us up the path, pausing with us on the two occasions we set the buckets down at leveled spots to catch our breaths. Despite the comparatively high temperature, the air seemed colder than usual in my lungs and I started breathing through a warming mitten. When I happened to glance again at the thermometer on the way past, the red line of alcohol had fallen another five degrees.

"I've some moose meat ground with beef fat from Joe and Claire Barkley's for hamburg tonight," I told my husband. "But what do you want tomorrow?"

"How's about another moose roast?" he asked. "That always makes the cabin smell so good."

"All right," I said, "but we'll have to saw it. There's still enough for a good roast in that last hind quarter. Want me to hold it for you?"

"That'll make it a lot easier, thanks."

I suppose the task took ten minutes, positioning the meat and manipulating the thin saw, which had a tendency to bend and bind. By the time I started indoors with the frozen block of meat and Brad had headed toward the oat pile to throw bundles to Cloud and Chinook, the temperature was 17° below zero.

The next morning the thermometer stood at 41° below zero. It was the weekly mail day of those earlier years, although ordinarily we stayed indoors as much as possible when the temperature was below 30° minus, Brad had to get off a survival article to meet a *Sports Afield* deadline. So one of us had to travel the total of five miles to and from town. When Brad proposed to go by himself, I objected.

"You've said that no one should be outdoors alone in weather this cold," I told him. "There's no telling what might happen."

"What could happen between here and the Hope?" he demanded. "Besides, if worse comes to worst, I can always stop and build a fire."

"I know, but I'd like to go, too," I told him. "It'd be a new experience."

"It will be an experience, all right," he said. "It'll be cold."

"I'll dress warm," I promised. "We can both wear our new Bauer goose-down underwear."

So we did. Over mine I drew on thick ski pants and a heavy woolen sweater, topping them with my long down jacket. Our feet, because they have the poorest circulation of any part of the body, were our primary concern. We each drew on two pairs of long woolen socks, topped by the soft, smoke-tanned, ankle-high moosehide moccasins made by the Indians at Moberly Lake, a day away across the ridge to the south. Then to keep out the snow, we each pulled on another pair of high woolen socks, oversized so that they would not constrict, and over them a larger pair of Indian moccasins.

Brad, who never wore a hat, clamped on a light pair of earmuffs. I knotted on a yellow woolen kerchief, one Brad had bought for me during our courting months around Essex on Massachusetts' lovely Cape Ann. We each wore two pairs of mitts.

"Shall we walk or take Cloud and Chinook?" I asked.

"It might be better to ride," he said. "Then we won't work up a dangerous sweat, breaking trail in the fresh snow. The exercise will do the cayuses good, too."

"Those saddles will be pretty cold."

"We'll be warmer riding bareback," Brad said. "And instead of subjecting them to those cold bits, I'll run a couple of lines from their halters. They neck-rein, anyway, so those will be as good as bridles and a whole lot more comfortable."

Cloud's heavy coat felt soft and warm between my knees, but even with that I was cold from the first. I kept feeling my face; when a portion started to become wooden, I cupped a bare warm palm over it until it was tingling again. Yet I never shivered as I would have on a much warmer day in Boston. Here the cold was dry, and it was around you and not inside you.

For all my garb, I might as well have been wearing burlap, so freely did the frigidity seep to every portion of my body. My breath, freezing as it streamed from my nose and mouth, rustled about me like silk. Brad's eyebrows and his dark brown hair, where it fell over his forehead, became white with frost. Long icicles attached themselves to Bushman's muzzle.

It was a virgin, trackless world. Not even red squirrels were scampering along their customary paths among the lodgepole pines and the blue spruce. Only where our passage knocked snow from branches overhanging the trail was there any sign on the white floor except for the marks of our animals' feet. The snow, granular with frigidity, crunched like gravel. When I sought to lift a sagging green poplar branch out of my way, it snapped in my hand like an icicle.

The smokes of Hudson Hope were soon ahead of us, then all around, but we could see no one stirring. The thermometer on the post office window stood at 43° below zero. Vesta Gething, the postmistress at that time, seemed surprised to see us and insisted that we come into the kitchen for cups of tea before we headed back with our sack full of mail. We accepted gladly, warmed as much by the northern hospitality as by the seething orange pekoe.

"You should put your horses in our barn," King Gething invited. His brother Larry nodded.

"Thanks, but we're heading right back," I said. "We want to get home before it gets any colder."

"Yes, it looks as if the temperature is really going down this time," King agreed. "You'll be careful of fire, of course."

"Fire?" I repeated.

"Yes," he said, "that's what causes most of the accidental deaths in the North, not cold."

The extreme cold manifested itself sooner on the way back. I followed Brad's example, sliding off of Cloud's back and leading him down the already broken trail. My feet seemed as heavy as clogs of ice, but they still had feeling, so I knew they were all right. My chest hurt. My ice-clogged nose would not admit enough air, so I began breathing with my mouth through the fleeciness of first one mittened hand, then the other. I revised my earlier estimation of wearing burlap. It was more like being clad in barbed wire. I wished I were back on the horse, but I was too stiff and heavily bundled to swing up by myself and too proud to ask Brad for help.

My body had started feeling numb, swathed and remote, no longer a part of my entity, although my awareness seemed sharper than ever. As I trudged laboriously and monotonously along the ceaseless trail, it seemed as if the unstained chasteness of that white world were gradually and enchantingly being condensed into my mind and perceptions.

The sky, above the frost ceiling, was a more intense azure than I had ever witnessed before, the snow a more gleaming white.

Trees no longer straggled away in a perplexing, blurring convergence. Where formerly there had been only snow and hoarfrost and sky, all now blended, separate and yet united, limitlessly intricate but still limitlessly pure and clear. I felt and viewed and scented all these details not as parts but as a whole: all at the same time, all as one.

Then we were back home. After letting the horses loose in their pole corral and throwing each a pair of bundles, I carried the mail into the cabin and stoked up the fires while Brad took the ax and pails down to the river for water. I made no move to doff my outer clothing, except for snow-covered socks and moccasins which would have worsened my condition by melting. Then Brad came back and he was helping me, rubbing life back into my arms and legs once more. I was a human being again, instead of a half-frozen clump.

The familiar sounds, after the silent miles of cold, began reasserting themselves: water steaming from our huge teakettle, the crackling fires, the click of Bushman's claws on the plank floor. There were the familiar smells, too: brisk coffee, crisp bacon, sourdough bread baked that morning, the sharp sweet scent of creosote dripping from the stovepipe as the solids in the smoke froze in the outside cold, the aroma of *Vol de Nuit* which I dabbed behind each ear in a spasm of voluptuousness. I was warm. I was happy. Looking out through a rift in an ice-encrusted window at the frost-spangled brittleness of the day, Brad's head next to mine, I felt I'd never been more contented with life.

Bushman was seated on his bear rug, tearing with sharp white teeth at the clogs of ice—hair and all—that had built up between his toes.

"Shall we look at our mail?" Brad inquired, starting to sort it into three piles: those for me in one, for him in another and for both of us in a third. As he took care of most of the never-ending correspondence with people who wrote us after reading one or another of his books, he received far more mail than I did. Because of that I was also allowed to open the third heap.

There was the usual deluge of encouraging fan mail and Brad would answer each letter personally. There were big New York checks from *Sports Afield* and *Field & Stream*, as well as a substantial, if smaller, one from *The American Rifleman* in Washington, D.C.

The publisher of Brad's last two books reported that his next royalty payments would set new records for him and asked for another, a modern and up-to-date *Wilderness Cookery*.

At least we were now self-sufficient and, living to a large extent off the country, we were even building a bank account. Our present-day experiment in repeating Thoreau's experiences was proving it would still work in this age of spacecraft and split atoms. What it all amounted to was that living this way gave us the spare time—which neither of us could have enjoyed back in the city where, though moderately successful, we'd always had to run just to keep even—to do the things we had always wanted most.

A personal letter from Jack Otis, a Boston friend, enclosed a newspaper clipping: COLD GRIPS THE HUB, read the headlines, *Zero by Midnight*.

I had another look at our thermometer. It was already down to 51° below zero and showing no inclination of stopping its plunge. We decided this was one of those nights we needed to keep a fire going in the airtight heater.

The western horizon that midafternoon became blotted in gray cotton wool. A brief frenzy of wind followed the oncoming darkness, driving smoky plumes of snow against the windows like chilled shot. The air momentarily became so dense with the swirling powder that when I watched Brad venturing outdoors again for more blocks of wood he was visible only as a shadowy form. He weaved with the load, especially when his woodheaped arms gave the unexpected gale more substance against which to hurl itself.

The unusual turbulence soon gave away again to stillness. When we got ready for bed later than usual because of some mysterious inner excitement, the thermometer had dipped another eight degrees.

We arose in darkness the next morning, stoking the heater as soon as we had dressed beside its remaining warmth, then dropping a match into the makings ready as usual in the cookstove. Brad turned the flashlight on what we now realized was a frail thermometer, to find that the colored line of alcohol had shrunk to 60° below zero.

The night was now clear, however, and the moon was a tilt of gold in the sky, alive with a multitude of pinpricked stars and the first faint fluttering of the Aurora Borealis. My spirits were high for some reason. While Brad was replenishing the wood supply, I jogged out to heave oat bundles to the whinnying Cloud and Chinook. Bushman followed me like a gray wraith and, eloquently holding up one paw and then another as he soon waited by the door, was as ready as I was to reenter the warmth of the cabin.

The world sparkled in the moonlight. Plumes of smoke from the two stovepipes rose like unsubstantial pillars to support a scintillating ceiling of frost that lay in luminous crystals above the booming earth. I thought of what I had read during my city days about the so-called eternal northern silence. Yet the cracking ground and the deeply-freezing live trees thundered with cold. There was the noise of ice shifting in the ever-flowing river, as if the relatively untried door of the new year were squeaking on its hinges. I wondered what Henry David Thoreau, once snug far to the south on Walden Pond in what he called "merry snowstorms," would have made of all this.

Daylight started as a band of white cold along the south-southeastern horizon, followed at long last by the red rim of an atmosphere-enlarged sun, like a glowing Christmas tree bauble. Against it, like a frosty cobweb, was a skein of birch and poplar branches, heavied with chaste inches of snow. Each separate twig had its ermine covering, all bright with a glaze of pale, smooth pink as the day started coming alive again.

There was an undercurrent of excitement in the air that kept Brad's typewriter clacking at top four-fingered speed, at work on the woodcraft book he was writing. Near the stove I kept busy with a frenzy of cooking. Although we did not boast an indoor thermometer, there must have been a difference of thirty degrees between the two parts of the small cabin. Brad worked in down underwear, heavy woolen trousers, two pairs of woolen socks, insulated boots and thick red woolen shirt while, perspiring in my kitchen, I tried to keep cool in moccasins, slacks and just a bra.

"I hope no one bursts in on us," I said with a laugh. "They'd think I'm crazy."

"No one will," he reassured me. "Nothing, not even fur, is traveling in weather like this."

"We were yesterday," I told him.

"That was an emergency," he said. "Never again."

Yet there was an exhilarating coziness here in our niche in eternity, with all we needed snugly about us.

With the sun on it, the thermometer warmed to minus 47° for a short time that noon. The day seemed even warmer, for the fires of life yet burned in the spruce and the lodgepole pine, wherein the sap rose. It was during this warmest part of the day that we walked down to the river with ax and dipper to get our daily three buckets of water.

Then came night once more, with everything a different degree of darkness, starting with the brighter sky and river and ending with the trees and the brownish cabin. The Northern Lights came out soon after sunset. Going outdoors to empty the accumulated dishwater of the day, I saw them first.

"Look, Brad," I called to him.

Overhead in the north, toward the back of our wilderness home, a huge drapery stretched from north to south, its folds luminescent with colors, chatoyant green predominant. This drape, like a giant stage traveler, shimmered as if it were made of heavy silk, each thread catching the light. What seemed to be bunch lights from the wings shot across the expanse like search-lights.

Then it was as if the traveler were opening. Stars appeared again in its center. Waves of luminosity pulsed on both sides, as if the heaviness of the curtain were being undulated by its move-ment and by drafts from the offstage wings. In the north, this drape came down to meet the snow, which was different shades of silvery gray rather than white as one might have expected.

The south-north streaks became red and purple but mainly green, as if some divinity were spinning color wheels. More and more stars winked into view until, all at once, the drapery vanished entirely; nothing was left but the cloudless, immaculate heaven with its thousands of stars glimmering through the scrim of frost-haze.

"Wasn't that wonderful?" Brad said in a voice so low that it seemed to stop at my ears. "It must have been one of the special rewards for those of us who are fortunate enough to travel to distant places."

"It's just like standing behind the scenes," was the way I summed it up.

Sixty-six degrees below zero! Ninety-eight degrees below freezing! The temperature fell that low the third day and I wondered if the theory that the world had reached some climax was true: if we were slowly and irretrievably moving toward another Ice Age.

Now it was hard to believe that the last of these tremendous sheets of ice that engulfed the northern half of North America—

in crystalline cold a mile thick—did not melt back and free the land until some twelve thousand years ago. At that time, when a notable part of the waters of the world were frozen, a broad land bridge existed where there is now a shallow sea between Alaska and Siberia. Ancestors of our moose and many other animals, followed by human hunters, crossed the land bridge from Asia— to Alaska, which for some reason was still fertile.

With the eventual receding of the ice, these ancestors of the North American Indian followed the rivers southward and eastward, a major egress perhaps having been the Peace River. In fact, one summer we accompanied an American Museum of Natural History anthropologist, Dr. Froelich Rainey, on a trip along the Peace. He sought the caves where these early aborigines may once have tarried. The most promising caves, it turned out, were along the river frontage of our original homesite.

Four times at least in the past million and a half years, glaciers swept southward across North America, then retreated. They scratched the signs of their progress: ploughing vast quantities of earth and rock ahead of them and damming existing rivers; scooping out basins which became, among others, our Great Lakes; and in other places heaping up hills. It is believed that our present twenty-two-mile-long Rocky Mountain Canyon cut its way around Bullhead Mountain. The former, more direct, channel—where the twelve-mile-long portage road now ribbons—had become clogged with debris. As a matter of fact, the supposition is that the huge spring gushing out of the ground at Hudson Hope is all that remains of the original stream.

I wondered what it had been like with such cold continuing for year after year. But the comparison, I realized, was not a valid one: such a sea of ice had stripped off all vegetation ahead of it, covering all the food that the grazers and the browsers sought. It drove them on ahead, the predators along with them, while without insects or seeds or nectar the birds had gone, too—until there was no sound but that of the wind and the shifting ice. Were we coming back to this again? Was this cold spell perhaps the start?

It was such thoughts, perhaps, that filled me with unease. It was hard to concentrate on anything. When I mixed sourdough bread, I almost forgot to leave out a cupful of the batter for the next starter. Brad, I noticed, moved from one task to another, rearranging books on the shelves behind his typewriter and in the storage

top: The new cabin in Rocky Mountain Canyon, two and a half miles upriver from Hudson Hope.

above: Laundry day.

A trout, fresh caught at our doorstep.

room, putting a fresh edge on his Randall knives, resharpening fishhooks while he was at it, and plaiting a rawhide riata on which he had been working.

It wasn't until we had been down to the river for the day's water and had tasted the comfortable contrast between the outside frigidity and our indoor tranquility, that we both settled down. Our typewriters resumed their steady rhythm, words and ideas tumbling forth in a stimulated torrent, as if we'd drunk a dozen cups of coffee. The sun, when it finally came out, flashed across the snow like an explosion of platinum fire.

"Catch the pace of the seasons," Thoreau had advised; "have leisure to attend to every phenomenon of nature, and to entertain every thought that comes to you."

Whereas summer was languid, winter sped on its way. It was almost with regret that I saw a sundog, like a strip of disembodied rainbow, in the sky that afternoon, for it almost surely meant the period of intense cold was coming to an end.

I wondered if, when the winter season broke up outwardly as it would be doing all too soon, it would do the same thing inwardly; if, by keeping my inner time in tune with outer time, I would feel the frost coming out of me, feel that I was heaving like the roads as the ice and snow within me dissolved, too.

10

Chinook

A whine from Bushman, scratching in the moonlit quiet of the night, awoke us. Then he began barking so violently that we both got up for a look around. His nose was applied to a crack in the door. Looking through the front window, we saw a moose cow and her long-legged calf crossing by the woodpile and heading up the hill to the kinnikinic-greened plateau to our west.

"Game is moving again," Brad said, "It must be warming up."

Sure enough, when we went out on the porch and turned the white cone of the flashlight on it, the thermometer, showed the temperature had risen to 18° below. Brad let the glinting light, sliding across the snow like a peppermint lozenge, touch the fresh tracks. Beside them, on the bitter green bark of a small poplar, were the white blazes made by hungry teeth. The stillness of the night, the Aurora-brightened sky and the fading moon, the stars burning like little platinum fires, the cold air with its elusive scent of snow and of cottonwood smoke and of the nearby corral, combined to envelop us in mystery and silence. My soul filled with yearning for the sun's coming splendor.

Then I heard a faint rushing sound, as of winds several hundred feet above the frozen ground. When a cloud moved with misty radiance across the moon, it was scudding from west to east.

"Sounds like a chinook up above us," Brad told me. "I only hope it comes down before it blows itself out."

Snow crystals glittered between us and the silver ribbon of river, as bright in the velvet darkness as planets. It gave every sign of being about to blossom into a beautiful day. The time, when Brad consulted the phosphorescent dial of the Rolex Explorer wristwatch I'd given him for Christmas, proved to be nearly six o'clock.

"Too late to go back to bed," I agreed, returning with him indoors. "You start the fire in the cookstove and I'll make us a feed of sourdough flapjacks. I started the batter working last night."

"It's a deal," he agreed enthusiastically.

Dudley Shaw had given us our original sourdough starter half a dozen years before.

"Fourteen years old," Dudley had then announced proudly. "Just started nicely."

That did make it comparatively young, I had learned later. Some of the sourdough starters in this part of the North had been begun during goldrush days at the turn of the century when, proving to be the only breadstuff that would surely rise under any condition short of freezing, it had become so popular that it had given the oldtimers their nickname: *sourdoughs*.

I'd had a lot of trouble with my log-cabin bread at first, following for awhile Thoreau's equally desperate suggestion, "It was fit that I should live on rice, mainly." Fortunately for my pride and our then empty pocketbooks, our appetites during our first joint taste of wilderness living were so robust that nearly everything tasted delectable.

Sourdough, which saved us from a daily diet of rice, is the first raising agent ever used in bread making. The primitive leavens contained wild yeasts, as well as numerous kinds and types of bacteria. If desirable organisms gained supremacy, the particular leaven was a success. If the fermentation was dominated by undesirable organisms, the product was inferior. Dudley's starter had, however, proved itself.

Starters occasionally lose their vigor, we discovered, particularly in the sort of cold weather we had been experiencing. Oldtimers then revive them sometimes with a tablespoon of unpasteurized cider vinegar. This puts new acetic acid bacteria on the job. A tablespoon or two of raw sour milk or cream, or of unpasteurized buttermilk or cultured sour cream, will get the lactic acids functioning again.

Your sourdough starter should never be stored in a warm place for very long. Heat encourages organisms harmful to yeast to grow at an extremely rapid pace. These soon gain sufficient control to produce putrefactive changes, the reason for some of the unpleasant smells one occasionally encounters in old starters in the north country. Another result is that the starter then becomes progressively weaker in dough-fermenting ability. The sometimes necessary solution? Begin a new starter.

Learning all that we had about sourdough, we decided to put it to some commercial advantage and Brad got in touch with the people at Chuck Wagon Foods at Micro Drive in Woburn, Massachusetts. Their dried foods for campers, hunters, fishermen, explorers and plain outdoor folk had early proved themselves to our satisfaction. They developed a dried sourdough mix with a booklet of recipes from Dudley's traditional concoction that sells by mail and in stores for a dollar as the *Bradford Angier Sourdough Mix.*

All that any housewife has to do is add flour and water only, and she'll have her own leavening agent for life. This starter, unless temporarily kept dormant by being dried or frozen, should be so fed about once a week. If you're regularly cooking with the starter, this process will take care of itself.

We have only one suggestion. The best flour for sourdough bread and biscuits is unbleached white, hard, winter wheat flour. Where you live, you may have to seek it in specialty gourmet and health stores. The all-purpose flour available in most grocery stores will not give such delicious, nutritious breads and biscuits, although it is fine for the flapjacks I was preparing for our breakfast this morning.

"How are they coming along?" Brad asked me now.

"Sumptuously," I replied.

A lot of fishermen, campers and other frequenters, of the farther places don't figure they've started the day right until they have stoked up with a stack of hot, tender, moist sourdough flapjacks. These flippers, as the sourdoughs often call them, are so easy to prepare that there's no need for the greenest tenderfoot to be dependent on store mixes. They're so tasty and wholesome, furthermore, that many a vacationer sniffs eagerly for more when shut in again by city streets.

I'd started enough for a couple of breakfasters the night before, adding two cups of flour and two cups of lukewarm water to my sourdough starter. I'd wrapped this mixture in a bowl and set it in our second room not too far from the heater. Now I returned the original amount of the starter to its scalded earthenware container, something you always have to do no matter what recipe you're using. That's always your next starter.

To the remaining batter I added two eggs, a tablespoon of sugar, one-half teaspoon salt, one teaspoon baking soda, one teaspoon warm water, and two tablespoons liquid shortening. Mix the eggs, sugar and salt with a fork. Dissolve the baking soda in the tea-spoon of warm water. Then stir all these into the batter, along with—in my case—not cooking oil, but melted bear fat.

If your flapjack batter seems a bit thick to pour easily, thin it with just enough milk. Flour, on the other hand, will provide stiffening. But if the batter is on the thin side, I find, the flippers will be more tender. I decided that this time mine was just right.

My heavy iron frypan was already hot, so I greased it sparingly with bacon rind, moving it further back on the stove so that the metal would not get hot enough to smoke. I turned each flapjack only once, when the hotcake began showing little bubbles. The second side took about half as long to cook.

"Ready?" I asked.

"I'm so hungry," he said, "that my stomach thinks my throat's cut."

"Here's the margarine. How's about some of Dudley's 'maple syrup'?"

"That will be exactly right," he said.

We began eating, and it was like listening to the Tchaikovsky Fourth, not only with our ears but with our palates.

In some ways this provocative syrup seemed even more remarkable to me this morning than the old, chipmunk-eyed trapper's original fourteen-year-old sourdough starter. It was certainly more incredible. In these days of soaring inflation and dwindling supplies from the northern New England maple groves, it could prove the answer for a lot of city people, too. Why not try it for yourself some rainy day?

Peel six medium-sized potatoes. Boil these uncovered in two cups of water until but one cup of fluid remains. Remove the vegetables, for use any way you want. Stirring the liquid until it reaches the boiling point again, slowly add one cup of white sugar and one cup of brown sugar. Once this has entirely dissolved, take the pan off the heat to cool slowly.

"Ghastly concoction," the old mountain man who gave me the simple formula nodded agreeably when, the initial time around, I first sampled the elixir at this primary stage. "Like home brew, it has to be aged in a dark place. After a couple of days in a bottle it'll be noble."

See if the first spoonful you doubtfully try doesn't appear to justify your worst suspicions, too. But bottle the syrup and tuck it away in a cabinet for several days to mature. Taste it again at the end of that time and see if you are not pleasantly amazed.

We were still amazed that morning. The flavor was almost beyond comparison, a phantom bouquet that haunted our tastebuds; something to be savored very deliberately and lingeringly. It tasted to us now exactly like prime maple syrup and we'd both been reared in maple syrup country. As Oscar Wilde remarked, it'll put you in the mood to pick your teeth with the spire of a cathedral.

Brad smiled, and there at the picture window with the table between us I was smiling back. Then before I knew it, the smile stirred into a little laugh. Abruptly he was laughing, also, and we sat across from one another over our steaming breakfast while our laughters mixed and became one. I heard the pleasure of it, merry, warm and understanding, in the lantern-hissing stillness. Then as suddenly as it had started, it was lost in more appetite-fulfilling mouthfuls and the silence ebbed back again.

The chinook continued for the next few days, frustratingly overhead, while temperatures on the ground averaged 30° below zero. This was about the minimum for outdoor comfort, but even then we confined our walking and riding to a minimum. All that springlike warmth so close overhead, but unreachable, thwarted us.

Then the fourth morning we awoke sweltering in our sleeping bags. There was a strange pattering; it wasn't until I got up and looked that I realized it was water running from our eaves. The boom of the wind no longer seemed to roar from high above, rather it came from every side—over my hair-tossed head and about my slippered feet and from all around me. Its moaning hollowness almost seemed to be vibrating within the pole pillars of the perch where I stood, watching it catch and straighten Bushman's tail.

Warm west wind, making the moonlit river its shining trough, was curling and twisting the melted snow from our roof in radiant ribbons. Some of the drops spattered on me and, being ice water, it was stinging cold. Instinctively I recoiled, bumping into Brad, who had appeared behind me and was trying to read the thermometer over my shoulder.

"Ooops," I said. "Excuse me. But isn't it wonderful?"

"Why, it's more than 50° above already," he said, throwing his arms around me while Bushman, running in a big circle and leaping drifts and bushes, barked. "What do you want to do today, Vena?"

"What about that new book you're working on?"

"I couldn't concentrate with all this going on, could you?" he said, holding me closer; two bodies and two voices in the warm embracing silence of the wilderness night. "Besides, Vena, there will be plenty of days to work."

"Let's explore as far south as we can across river," I said.

"All right," Brad agreed. "We'll just take our .22 and the tea pail and make our lunch off the country."

"Wonderful," I said.

The quadruple mischiefs of blackness, melting, slipperiness, and wind built up before sunrise. The south-southeastern sky was lighting up slowly with a pallid saffron radiance when we started out with Bushman. Everything else was dwindling shades of blue, the densest hues of which suffused the river canyon like liquid dye. Part of it was reflected in Brad's eyes, which seemed bluer than ever.

The footing of the slope down to the river was tricky and Brad took my hand. We left the empty water buckets, ax and dipper on the ledge, to be carried up upon our return home. Then Brad and I each picked up a long, dry spruce pole. We never ventured on the frozen Peace without one, for then if we should ever break through the ice, the pole could be reasonably expected to bridge the gap and afford a means of escape.

"Oh, can we explore the islands first?" I asked.

"Why not?" Brad said. "We have to go by them, anyway, and later on we won't be able to get out there except in a boat."

"We should have a boat here."

"I've been thinking about building one," he told me.

Three islands were opposite the cabin, each with a character of its own. Nearest our sunny north shore was a small, high knoll of an islet whose sheer sides looked impossible to scale without a rope. Several gnarled trees on top thrust up their stunted limbs. Along the rocky sides were hundreds of gourdlike jugs of mud, the nests of the colonies of brightly hued cliff swallows who would be swooping back in a few months.

Ahead of them, though, would be the Canada geese, piercing the heavens like joined Indian lances. We knew from past springs, when Dudley had lived here, that several pair of them nested on the elevated but easily scaled island in midriver, just below our new home. Then directly opposite our fifty acres, cut from both shores by rapids, was a long, low, thickly timbered bulwark. Its now snow-covered gravel bar, I imagined, would be well worth working if individuals could ever sell their gold on the world market.

Just as along the river shores, the ice was smoothest directly next to each island. This was because the Peace never entirely froze. When temperatures dropped lower than usual, as during the days just passed, the channels beneath the surface clotted with jamming ice, forcing water to the top as overflow. Then there was the water that spread over the surface when chinooks melted the snow, and there was the water from the eternally flowing creeks and springs. All this sought the lowest levels; where the Peace River was consistently lowest was along its sun-reflecting banks.

The ice, too, had been heaving and buckling all winter, so the ribbony flatnesses extended in other directions, following dells among the ridges and hummocks and there forming enticing mazes along which one could have skated. Bushman explored some of these, but for once our rubber-shod feet had better traction than his rasping claws. When he bounded over the rough surface he wasn't much better off, for then he had to beware of deep cracks and patches of hollow crust.

"Get away from there, Bush!" I called when he loped close to an open rent of cascading water.

It was some two hundred yards across the Peace at that particular point and the ochre-stained shale cliffs on the opposite shore reflected my voice. Bushman had started in our direction. Now he hesitated, head cocked, and turned back. When he did frisk toward us, I yelled again for the fun of it and the echo took him to the other shore, romping and barking.

We turned toward still another island downriver, a small but tall, oddly shaped projection that had so eroded that it was broadest at its top. Dudley Shaw had named it Teapot Island and the name was apt. Again, there was no way to get to the top.

There were two more islands, one of them opposite the Hope, but we felt no urge to go that far downriver. Instead, we turned inland opposite the cabin, following a frozen creek. This led up through a poplar flat and soon into a beaver meadow behind a long, low dam. Cut green poplars were along the shore, the low stumps chewed round and around the way a beaver does, never knowing which way his tree will topple.

The green bark on a number of the fallen trunks was gouged by moose teeth; enormous moose tracks were frozen in what had been slush covering the pond. Three huge brown mounds, beaver houses of sticks and mud, arched from the icy surface. Willows grew from and around these, and the moose had been nipping at these, too.

"Look, pussy willows," I said. Sure enough, a number of the fleecy little gray ovals were already forming on the red wands. "Let's pick some on the way back. What's that narrow slit that has been cut up that hill to the left?"

"It's the old Peace River Block Line," Brad told me, "the line marking the three-and-one-half million acres of arable land that British Columbia deeded to the Dominion of Canada in 1883. It was the province's contribution toward construction of the Canadian Pacific Railway. The animals have made a game trail of it here."

"Won't it be easier traveling that way?" I asked.

"I suppose so," he said, "a lot of the way, anyhow. It'll keep us moving in a straight line, at least. It runs nearly north and south. As you know, it forms the eastern boundary of our new fifty acres."

We climbed a steep slope out of the old river channel, up through small spruce, flushing a grouse on the flat above, which Brad shot in the head as it perched high in an old cottonwood. Soon afterward we passed the remains of an ancient cabin and in the overgrown clearing Brad got a second grouse. We had the nucleus of our lunch.

"See our cabin down there, across river," he said, handing me the binoculars.

They were ten power, with a 5.5° field, and it was almost as if we were in our yard. The sun had finally shown itself in a million sparkles over the white incline of snow behind us and, standing boldly in its brightness, our home stood out like a sturdy brown block in the tumultuous blue air. The way the light was slanting down through the trees reminded me of being back in Paris in the memorable early morning serenity of the Bois.

"See Bullhead there to the left," he said. "The way it's hidden from the cabin and from Hudson Hope, it's hard to realize it's so close, like a protective guardian. We really live on its east flank."

We did not reach the crest of our particular incline until noon and there ahead of us, to the south, was the azure gleam of a small lake. We'd counted an even dozen deer and two moose on the way up, a long-legged lynx who sat and regarded us for a long moment before padding unhurriedly away, quite a few grouse—some of whom exploded unnervingly from almost beneath our feet—many chattering red squirrels and innumerable varying hares. Now Bushman caught one of the latter for his lunch.

"Getting hungry, Vena?" Brad asked me.

"Uummm."

"Why don't we eat here, then? There're plenty of highbush cranberries and rose hips around for dessert, and here's a stand of Labrador tea. That's one of the nicest things about snow in the woods. You can dine anywhere you want. No worry about water."

We harmlessly tore enough fluttering wisps of birch bark from the nearby trees to start a fire with one match and soon had a poplar blaze burning away to coals. Brad slanted a green pole over an edge of the campfire and from that I suspended our tea pail.

Besides having a surprisingly low water content, snow acts like a blotter on its meltage: stirring, I melted several inches of water in the bottom of the can before I filled it with pieces of ice crust. I had to add more chunks of this crust from old storms before a full can of water bubbled merrily.

It's easy to distinguish Labrador tea, also known as Hudson's Bay Tea over much of the North, where the oldest trading corporation in the world still maintains its red-roofed white trading posts. It is a pretty evergreen shrub whose robustly aromatic leaves make it one of the more famous wild teas on this continent. It is found growing densely in woods, muskegs, swamps, damp mountain meadows and across the tundras of Alaska and Canada—south to New England, Pennsylvania, New Jersey and the Great Lakes states, where it is seen mainly in mountain bogs. Its leaves were among those our forefathers gathered for tea during the American Revolution.

This member of the heath family is easy to distinguish. It's a resinous evergreen shrub ranging from one to four feet high, so attractive that two centuries ago the English brought it to the British Isles to embellish their home gardens. The telltale features are the alternate, dry, leathery, fragrant leaves whose smooth edges roll inward toward densely woolly undersides. These underneaths darken from grayish to reddish brown, as the otherwise green leaves age. These distinctive, thickish leaves are usually less than two inches in length, although some of those we used today were twice as long. Brad dropped a palmful, about the same amount as he'd have used of oriental tea, into the simmering water, then set this aside to steep.

"It'll be fine in about five minutes," he promised me. "In the meantime, let's get our grouse started."

It took only minutes to pluck and clean and two birds. We spitted each on a separate green stick, slanted these over the cherry-red coals and turned them from time to time. Meanwhile, we roasted the livers, hearts and the cleaned gizzards.

"If you'll watch all this," Brad said, "I'll get us some berries."

The sizzling meat, gnawed away from the bones as trees creaked and bushes rattled in the balmy west breezes that ardently embraced us here on this hillside, had a taste of luxury to it that made the enchanted world all about seem more real. All too soon, it was time for dessert.

Everyone is familiar with rose hips, the seed pods of the roses that grow wild almost everywhere in Canada and the United

States where the soil is sufficiently moist. Few of us are aware, however, that three of this small fruit have as much vitamin C as an orange. We don't pay much attention to these free vitamins in the States and those parts of Canada where oranges are not too expensive, but in England during World War II, some five million pounds of rose hips were gathered from roadsides and put up to take the place of scarce citrus fruits. Dried and powdered, these cousins of the apple are sold in Scandinavian countries for use in soups, for mixing with milk or water to make hot and cold drinks, for spreading over cereals, etc., all of which they do admirably. This noon we just cut each in half, removed the central core of seeds and relished the remainder raw.

The juicy red highbush cranberries, with their unusual and never-to-be-forgotten sweetish sour flavor, usually take an acquired taste, but we had acquired this long ago. In fact, I thought, as I let the sherbetlike juice of these melt on my tongue, I wouldn't swap the provocatively different jelly they make for any other in the world.

I remembered Thoreau's more conventional cranberries, which he described as "small waxen gems, pendants of the meadow grass, pearly and red." The highbush cranberry of the North—which grows from Alaska to Labrador and Newfoundland, south through Canada and the northern States—is really a *viburnum*, although in Hudson Hope we have real cranberries, too. I usually put up a few jars of them each fall.

Thoreau had also said, "I learned that a man may use as simple a diet as the animals, and yet retain health and strength. Yet men have come to such a pass that they frequently starve, not for want of necessaries but for want of luxuries." Living off the country as we were this noon, I also reflected on that.

It was even warmer that afternoon on the way home. Snow, no longer like gravel, was soft under our boots. Loose bark fluttered on the birch trees. The emerald needles of the conifers rustled. Gray Canada jays, squeaking happily, swooped from branch to branch just ahead of us. A small flock of snowbirds, now white with winter, scattered through a gaunt stand of cottonwoods like hurled petals. Fresh wildlife tracks of all sizes were everywhere.

Chinooks, I decided, were one of the more pleasant parts of the energizing subarctic winters. Starting as warm damp winds from the Japanese Current off the Alaska Panhandle, those here were additionally warmed by losing part of their wetness in the Coast

Range. Sweeping down the eastern side of those heights, they were compressed and heated even more. By the time the snow-eaters, as the local Indians called them, reached Hudson Hope they were as mild as spring zephyrs.

As the winter-shortened day became full of dusk, empressed with the mystery that lives at the core of all loveliness, swarming twilight gathered along the river and the mouths of the creeks and rolled like blue fog up the valleys, catching in the branches of the trees about us. The planet Venus pricked the azure southwest. The slopes of Bullhead were still bright as we descended into the deep blue, crossed the ice, filled our water pails and, pleasantly languid in the drowsy fragrance of Spring, puffed up the incline to the cabin. I went to throw bundles to the prancing horses, while Brad began carrying in firewood.

At this season we, like Thoreau, seldom had a visitor, but lived alone as snug as meadow mice. In fact, little wood mice—the cute Disney types with large ears and inquisitive noses—had been at one corner of our wooden box of dried apples in the smaller room. They had been lugging sweet segments to their lairs, along a well-trod tunnel in the snow that the chinook now laid bare. But the amount of fruit they took was small and did no harm, and they were welcome to it.

So in our winter seclusion we, and likewise the alert Bushman who barked sharply but soon stopped, were surprised by a merry "Cherrio." Hearing a stamping on our stoop, we opened the door to greet Dudley Shaw, still our nearest neighbor, living as he did between us and the major portion of the town.

"Noble chinook," Dudley said, eyes blinking amiably behind thick spectacles. He doffed his venerable felt hat and, hanging it on the handy thermometer which now registered 53°, entered at our invitation. "Glorious day for a powwow. Besides, Larry Gething sent you something."

When the old trapper took off his neat old brown mackinaw and tan packsack, he seemed smaller than ever. Bushman was flicking an oxford-gray tail and ducking his head beneath the visitor's long slender fingers.

"Bushman seems to be in bountiful spirits," the small man said in a voice that was not at all small. "Must be glutting himself with wapoose."

"Yes, we ate off the country across river yesterday," I said, "and that's what Bush had, a rabbit. They're everywhere this year. Will you have some tea, Dudley? You'll stay for lunch, of course."

"Some lap would be fine, thank you, Vena," Dudley said, unstrapping the canvas cover of his knapsack and taking out a package done up in brown paper. "Brought you lunch if you don't mind a bit of cooking."

"Thank you," I said, fumbling with the knot in the string. "Oh, what is it?"

"A young mountain goat blundered into one of Larry's snares up on Bullhead," Dudley said. "Ghastly. Noble eating, though. Larry sent you half a dozen chops. They're not very huge."

"Wonderful," I said. "That'll be two for each of us."

"Cheerful place, you've made this," Dudley approved, looking carefully around. "Joyous view. Where's your blinking heater?"

"We added on another room," Brad said. "It's over there through this door, Dud."

"Good idea. Women are notorious for needing more space than bachelors."

Brad laughed.

"Is there any special way you like these cooked?" I asked, spreading out the six well-trimmed chops which looked plump and tender.

"A sprinkling of marjoram before you consign them to the heat may help bring out the flavor," Dudley suggested diffidently. "But don't bog them down with it. About half a teaspoon should be glorious. This little rascal has been glutting himself with lichens and sweet grass, so he should cheer us up vastly. Some people think young mountain goat is best, sizzling hot, with some wild mint jelly."

"I've got just the thing," I said, turning toward the storage room. "I put it up last fall from the mint right up here on the flat and I've been saving if for just the right occasion."

Rubbed well with margarine and salt and a little pepper, then dusted with marjoram, the chops were delectable after being broiled on our wire grill, laid across an unlidded stovetop over open hardwood coals. They were still juicy and pink inside when I turned them onto our oven-heated stainless steel plates, along with mint sauce, mounds of fluffy mashed potatoes and sliced parsnips, the latter two from our root cellar.

The three of us sat by the picture window and relished every last morsel, while outside the balmy chinook breezes still blew, occasionally forcing puffs of smoke out through the seams of the creaking stovepipe. Then, after letting Bushman outdoors with the bones, we had some of my moose meat mince pie.

"Something like this," Brad decreed, "would make converts out of those who never taste the meal they're eating but are all the time thinking about the next."

"Noble crust," Dudley added, tasting its flakiness.

"I made it the way you showed me, with bear fat," I told him.

"Can't beat bear fat for shortening," Dudley said. "Thanks, Vena, I will have some more lap, please. Then I've got to ramble up the trail and see it there's any blinking plunder in my traps. How's the enemy?"

"The time?" I said. "It's nearly one o'clock."

"Ghastly," Dudley said, reaching for his jacket.

We walked out past the corral with our friend and watched him climb the hill to the flat behind the cabin, then with a wave of his hand, turn left upriver. The snow-devouring wind, which was decimating the drifts without even melting them, was so strong that for a moment it blew the curl out of Bushman's tail. It tangled my shoulder-length hair and I reached in my pocket for a scarf. Laundry, which gave every evidence of being already dry, having been washed in the softness of melted snow earlier, whipped on the line.

"This is much too good an afternoon to stay indoors," Brad said. "What do you want to do?"

"The last oranges I priced at the Bay were a dollar and sixty cents a dozen and they were little, miserly things. You said yesterday that tests have shown the vitamin C in the raw pulp of rose hips runs nearly 7000 milligrams a pound. What is it you need a day to stay healthy and keep from getting scurvy?"

"Oh, sixty to seventy-five milligrams," he said. "Rose hips are up to sixty times richer in vitamin C than even lemon juice and richer in iron, calcium and phosphorus than oranges. There's even vitamin E in the seeds."

"Then why should we waste any more money?" I wanted to know. "Let's spend the afternoon gathering rose hips. Then I can slice them in half, take out the core of seeds and dry the remaining shell in the oven for eating like raisins."

"There're lots of them all around," he said, catching my enthusiasm. "Let's get some paper bags."

"How can we get the vitamin E out of the seeds?"

"Vesta Gething was telling me that some wilderness wives grind them, boil them in a small amount of water, then strain them through a cloth. You can use the vitamin-teeming fluid in place of the water called for in syrups, jams and jellies."

"We're running low on highbush cranberry syrup for our pancakes," I said. "Let's pick some of them, too. Nothing's going to be squandered in this family."

It chinooked that day and the next, although by then the west wind had lost most of its intensity. That night I awoke to pull the kersey flap of my down sleeping bag higher around my shoulders. The warm westerly had passed.

11

Candle Ice

I came wide awake abruptly during a night two months later. I wondered why, because there seemed to be nothing astir but the deep breathing of Brad and the sleeping wolfhound. Then all of a sudden my husband was hunching up in his sleeping bag, too, and there was the rasp of Bushman's nails against the plank floor. But something else was with us in the night; a moving, an entity. As I strained my ears, an impellent, a pressure, an urging—rather than a noise—thrummed somehow deep within them, back into the convolutions of my mind.

It was not a definite noise but, rather, a distant stirring that throbbed softly, pervasively and continuously, urging rather than demanding a subtle attention. We both got up and went outside in our boots, Bushman slithering past us through the creaking door Cold didn't strike through our thin pajamas at first; it never did. Moonlight stretched about us, its stillness and that of the chill silver ribbon of river absorbing the mysterious tone that now lifted in volume, wavered, soared once more out of the silence and then lost itself in it.

We stood attentively several moments more, looking and listening, but there was no noise nor motion except for Bushman, who had joined us after a brief excursion afield and whose flailing tail beat at my chilled legs. Then we were back, shivering for the moment in the kersey fleeciness of our goose-down bags. Instantly, it was morning, glowing with the quiet, yet somehow glittering luster of a freshwater pearl.

"I wonder if the grizzly has been back at that moosehide?" I said across our flapjacks, Canada bacon and steaming coffee. "Can we ride up there and see?"

Brad was smiling and this morning his blue eyes didn't look at all icy.

"Spring getting to you, too?" he said. "Sure, I'll saddle up while you're doing the dishes."

Every April, when we first perceived a faint tinge of spring green in the poplar tops across river, we revived with nature, sensing that her victory was ours. The civilization we had left behind us seemed flat and stale by contrast and—during this season in particular—I never wanted to go back.

The ice along the shores of the Peace was beginning to candle in places, especially where earth and rock beneath it were becoming increasingly warm as the ice reflected the sunlight. Ice that has disintegrated into long vertical needles is called candle ice. More ardent suns and increasing chinooks were gradually melting the snow. The days were growing sensibly longer and at last we could see our way clear to getting through the rest of the cold season without adding to our woodpile, for fires in the heater were no longer necessary.

I'd long been alert for more signs of spring: the chance note of some arriving cliff swallow, the first tree frog's peep, or the initial striped chipmunk's chirp, for the stores of oats they had been tapping during breaks in their winter's drowse must now be nearly exhausted.

Brad and I were still gingerly crossing and traveling the river, although the rapids across the ledge in front of the cabin were now a racing dance of open water. The first two Canada geese had already returned and were basking long hours on the edge of the ice by the juncture of the two opposite islands; on the lower of these, they would soon be bringing up this year's goslings. I could see the two large birds now through the picture window, as we sipped our coffee.

"Hear that?" Brad said suddenly.

A thin, distant clamor impinged itself on the margin of the silence. Cups in hand, we went outdoors.

"Swans," Brad breathed.

We were both staring upward, surveying the lighting heavens, and we finally saw them above Rocky Mountain Canyon, so high that their beating wings caught the first glimmering dazzle of the sun. The swans were a rough, hyphenated V against the vault of the sky. We looked and listened as they vanished into the diluted light, even before the noise of their gabbling was gone. The sound still reached our ears, like a distant echo, after they had vanished upstream; most of the migrations here followed the Peace River east and west, rather than holding to the eventual north-south lines.

"Maybe that's what awoke us last night," I said.

"Maybe," he said doubtfully, "but it sounded too ominous for that."

I looked across river, again wishing that we had a boat for later on. For some reason, the opposite shore where no one yet lived continued to hold a fascination for me. I was constantly making for it, always with the sense of security that carrying a long dry pole gave me. The shore ice was overrun by rising water which further weakened it, but I found that once I had reached the solid core a few feet beyond land, I could proceed nearly anywhere by using caution and by testing ahead for candle ice. The end of a pole would drive through several feet of these ice needles at a single jab.

"We should really keep off the river," Brad had told me just the afternoon before.

"I'm being careful," I had told him. "We've never had any real trouble yet, not all these years, and in a little while we won't be able to get over there at all. You don't have to come with me."

"You don't think I want you going alone, do you?" he asked.

The river had become rusty and grimy, as what was left of the winter snows melted to reveal the accumulated dust from the cut-banks in the canyon. Spring rains lay, too, dull and corroding on its rotting splendor.

The pressure of the reawakening current built up within the

hidden channels until parts of the still resisting sheath swelled, burst and became tumbled masses of ice cakes. The intervals between these became frosted with ice particles, like white snow, which bulged in what looked like solid masses. Bushman, who'd been barking after a low-flying mallard, had leaped on one of these a few days before, believing it solid. He'd disappeared in an instant, but as soon as he bobbed up, Brad grabbed him by the collar and hauled him out, before he could be swept under the ice.

We trailed a long rope from his collar after that whenever we were venturing on the river, although he sagaciously never got into difficulty again.

The horses, whom Brad had saddled, turned to regard me as I crunched down the path to the corral. Their ears pricked up and they nickered softly. Brad was tightening the cinch on my gray gelding, Cloud.

"You didn't take long," he said, but Cloud whinnied long and shrilly, obliterating whatever it was he said next.

I extended a palmful of sugar for Cloud and another for Brad's sorrel mare, Chinook. Both accepted them gently, then Cloud began nuzzling the orange scarf I had knotted around my throat. I rubbed away his soft nose and he nipped at the silk with long, yellowed teeth.

"He's all yours," Brad said, handing me the tooled reins he'd bought me in Ensenada the winter before, when we'd been away from the woods for several personal reasons and had been incidentally doing some necessary university research on a new book. The horse started turning even before I'd swung into the saddle, planting his hind legs widely and dancing on them, forefeet lifted playfully.

Then Brad was astride the sorrel mare, who spiritedly leaped into the lead. She wanted to buck, but Brad held her alert head high and she settled down, as different from the gentle and reliable gray as any horse could be. I tried to bring Cloud alongside my husband, but Chinook kicked, then nipped, at the gelding, so I was content to ride single file for the first part of the trip at least.

Every leaf and twig this early morning were covered with sparkling ice armor. Even the kinnikinic on exposed stretches were hung with innumerable diamond pendants which jingled merrily when brushed by the horses' feet. It was literally the wreck of jewels and the crash of gems.

"Such is beauty ever—neither here nor there, now nor then," Thoreau had written, "but wherever there is a soul to admire. If I seek her elsewhere because I do not find her at home, my search will prove a fruitless one."

As we followed a riverside quarter mile of Dudley's trapping trail, where chinooks had swept all winter, an abrupt flurry of wind whipped brown poplar leaves from the forest floor, so that a flutter of them seemed to be chasing us.

A small flock of red-wing blackbirds appeared from somewhere, settling down ahead of us on swaying brown strands of grass before flinging themselves into the air again with liquid, gurgling song. Then a spruce grouse exploded under Chinook's feet and the sorrel lurched giddily sideways, almost from beneath Brad. But Cloud still ambled along steadily, refusing to become excited. I tried to heel the gray into a faster gallop, then resigned myself and fell back into following the flashier sorrel in a smooth canter that was as comfortable to sit as a rocking chair.

A sparrow hawk, the American kestrel, hovered toward us on rapidly beating blue-gray wings, his handsome black and white head shining. Then, when he seemed about to dive, he lifted almost upright in the wind for an extended moment before turning toward the hills. He and his mate would be having their young soon.

We finally tied the two horses the other side of Box Canyon where, at a point where the land sloped down to the river, we had camped that December night. Actually, the ice here seemed dangerous only along the shore. I thought we could pick our way up and down the river once we had reached the solid core in the middle. We cut particularly long, seasoned poles; being exceedingly cautious, I thought, if such an adventure could be termed cautious. I started across while Brad was still scraping his pole smooth.

A new rivulet, which had cut its channel atop the weakening ice, all at once barred my way. It wasn't deep and I was able to cross it on jammed ice cakes, wading a bit at the end. The well-oiled boots, softened with bear grease, kept my feet dry. Between me and the dark patch made by the abandoned hide of last winter's first moose—long since shedding its hollow brown-black hair—was a confusion of ever-crumbling and twisting cakes.

The ice on which I was standing suddenly seemed to be heaving and swelling beneath my rubber soles. From far up the canyon came, louder and more definitely rumbling, the strange whisper of sound that had awakened us the night before.

I started to turn back when the white-streaked ice about my feet quivered, started to disintegrate, and all of a sudden crumbled. With a shattering sound, a whole section of the river surface gave way beneath me. I was conscious of Bushman's barking and of the clattering, slamming, crashing, banging crescendo of the spring current.

The long pole in my hands bridged the gap in the river's surface; I clung to it with all my ebbing strength while agonizing cold cut at me, as if I were being slashed with icy knives. Emptiness and frigidity engulfed me like liquid air and a chill void lethargy swam in an all-encompassing wave throughout my body and mind. The shock of the icy water had driven the breath out of my lungs. I could feel the last flickering flame deep within my veins dwindling and ebbing away into the vicious deforming blankness of ice and sky.

For a moment, I felt only ever-number, ever-sicker despair. I thought, how could I have been such a fool? It had been only an instant, but already the river was gripping me with deeper, bone-chilling strength. My struggles seemed futile against the race of ice-charged water, swift here, which was striving to suck me beneath its sheath.

Gasping, I tried to kick my stiffening legs straight under me so that I could lever myself out. I ventured one hand off the pole to close on the edge of ice. This crumbled in my grip. I essayed again to lift myself on the pole. The best I could do was chin myself. Pretty soon, I realized, feeling my eyelids wavering and my muscles relaxing, I wouldn't even be able to do that; nothing but let myself sink into the cold icy abyss of nothingness.

Finally, with utmost effort, I did manage to get my breasts on the pole, which creaked under my weight. I tried again to kick free of the tumult. The current held me relentlessly in glacial claws, surging over the pole at one point, then smoothing again but never releasing its deadly pull.

I tried again, with my last feeble flame of energy, to come out of it. Then I felt something drag across my hands. It was the long rope attached to Bushman's collar. I grabbed hold of it in final desperation and then he was pulling at me, nails slipping on the ice. But, somehow, it was slowly making all the difference. Then I realized Brad was also there, flat on his stomach and pulling, too.

With sudden hope, like a searing flash, I felt the renewing tenseness of leaden tendons, the lessening constriction of my lungs and the savage pounding of my heart.

Kicking free of the race, finally, with one tremendous surge upward, I managed to roll away from the gap, where water was already swelling and spreading. Unsteadily, with Brad's help, I managed to stand.

"If it hadn't been for you . . . " My eyes were pulled back to the dark hole and I reached down for the end of the long pole that had also served me so well.

Something was pulling at me and I realized I still held the wolfhound's rope. The wind, plastering my wet clothes against my skin, increased my shivering. We were going to have to do something fast if I was to keep from freezing but, with growing lassitude, I relaxed in the thought that now someone else was going to take care of all that.

"Take my arm," Brad was saying. "Come on, honey."

Stumbling in my effort to follow his steadying advance, I was finding it hard to bend my knees. I couldn't understand why at first. Then I realized my garments were freezing. This shut out the insistent wind, but soon I would be encased rigidly in icy armor. The bout with the river had left me weak. More than once I had to sag my whole weight against Brad. I was breathing jerkily and each gulp of the frost-ridden air hurt my lungs. Then all we had to do was wade the last few feet.

I was on the snowy shore, fumbling with my buttons and trembling all over.

"Get undressed," Brad told me. "I'll have a fire going in a shake."

It was as dimly unbelievable as a dream. With huge strips of birch bark, in moments he had brought alive the roar of a fire, on which he piled whole dead evergreens. While the blaze was building its ardent boisterousness, I struggled out of my boots, then the rest of my ice-encased clothing. Brad rubbed me vigorously with his dry woolen shirt, then threw his down jacket over my shrinking shoulders.

"How do you feel?" he said tightly.

"F-f-f-fine."

"That was too close," he said, and then an inconsequential thought struck him and he gave a taut laugh. "You're so anxious to get across the river that we'd better build a boat this spring."

"Oh, c-c-c-can we?"

He clasped me to him, softly at first, then more tenaciously and more ardently, until he was pressing me against his body with an almost painful tenderness and ferocity. Then he held his head a little bit away, stared down at me and smiled. "I love you, Vena."

"I love you, too."

As we stood there in the great yellow gleam of the campfire, Shelley's verse flashed across my mind:

> *Nothing in the world is single*
> *All things by a law divine*
> *In one another's being mingle—*
> *Why not I with thine?*

At first, I couldn't get enough of the fire, I was quivering so. Later, when Brad had rearranged my garb as a wind shield, on nearby trees not too close to the flames, and my blood was coursing warmly again, he got the tea pail we always carried in a saddlebag. He scooped it full of the snowlike ice crystals which were pressing against this north shore. If drafts of coldness hadn't still been chilling me, it would have seemed like a picnic. Seeing me shiver anew, Brad threw more fuel on the blaze and sparks zigzagged against the soaring white-hooded nearness of Bullhead like fireworks.

The ice pack, its booming strangely muffled for the moment, seemed to be crushing closer and I wondered for an instant if Brad had built the fire too near to the bank. One of the horses whickered, then snorted. When I turned my eyes back to the river, a section of tormented ice broke free and then clogged again, crashed loose once more and then dammed itself anew.

Finally, with an exploding surge that caused both horses to whirl around and started Bushman barking, the Peace River hurtled free where we had just crossed. It became a dancing, azure-reflecting torrent in which glittering ice cakes spun, bobbed and cavorted.

A mighty roar throbbed through the wilderness. I was away from it. I was safe. Spring had arrived with a rush.

12

The Peacemaker

A strange tranquility, delicate as a bit of abalone shell long polished by the sand, settled over me during our ride home in dusk that soon closed about us, filling the forest with mystery. Not wanting to risk the unstable cutbanks, we cut back from the now invisible river that grumbled in the gloom. Then I saw it again, ebony and platinum and gold: white ahead where a rising full moon shimmered on its turbulence, yellow against the last rim of the sun as it set behind Bullhead with the slow magic of a northern twilight.

What was left of the sun gave us lean, El Greco shadows, like figures in a sandhill crane's dream. At the end of one of them I suddenly spied the suggestion of a narrow mask and, as it withdrew into the chill evening blackness, a bushy tail. Barking, Bushman disappeared in pursuit.

"See that fox?" Brad said excitedly. "With all the rabbits, it's a great year for them."

"I hope," I said with an effort, feeling weariness seeping like a slow sweet wine through my veins, "that Bush doesn't catch it."

"He'll give up first," Brad said. "He's anxious to get home, too."

Cloud's and Chinook's feet broke through crusted snow and crashed into ice-skimmed puddles I could not see, their hooves crunching along smartly now that they were on their way back to their oats. Wary of getting a branch in the eye, we had to hold them back, even my usually stolid gray.

The final red filigree of sun disappeared behind us, leaving Bullhead Mountain more a crouching than a towering guardian, covert and near at hand and somehow companionable. Ahead, pinpoints of stars were slowly appearing. I watched, scarcely moving in my saddle, as the chill sea of dusk ebbed westward, spreading its cold luminescence across the paling arch of the sky and the stilling air and the white-flacked wilderness below. Night, in this adorned and pregnant forest, was being born out of the silence of time and space.

"What'll we call this boat we're going to build?" Brad was asking.

"Well," I started; it was an effort to drag my mind away from the way the moon groped initially for the pine tops with gleaming, spatulate fingers before laying a flat, phosphorescent palm on the river. "Well, it's supposed to *make* the Peace. Why not call it The Peacemaker?"

"Perfect," he decreed.

We started work on The Peacemaker two mail deliveries later, with some douglas fir marine plywood and spruce two-by-fours that Les Bazeley brought from Fort St. John for us in his truck. We built it upside down on two log skids that Cloud and Chinook slid to a flat stretch in front of the cabin.

Charlie Ohland, a retired Swedish sailor and ship carpenter who had sailed all over the world, was the guiding spirit. The discovery of him was as rewarding as finding an old key that will turn a rusty lock. Charlie had just moved to Hudson Hope, with his Finnish wife Kay, to work at King Gething's coal mine and with our help he had bought Larry Gething's old Bullhead Mountain trap line. His broad hands reached his knees, and he had an oarsman's wrists and forearms. His strong, seamed face usually had the additional upturning lines of a smile.

Charlie, who walked with his feet far apart as if he were still on a pitching deck, hiked up the trail from Hudson Hope each morning. He and Brad worked together until dusk, hammering, sawing, planing, sanding, caulking and, finally, varnishing.

Kay, a fervent fisherman and already acclaimed as one of Hudson Hope's better cooks, accompanied him a lot of days and fished off the ledge in front of the cabin. On these occasions, we could usually look forward to sizzling meals of flaky rainbows, Dolly Varden and Arctic grayling, while her night lines often brought in succulent ling.

If you catch a good mess of ling—freshwater codfish that visiting scientists have told us are living fossils—and want to serve up something special for company, get a couple of frypans heating. In the first, Kay showed me, fry the large vitamin-rich livers very lightly in butter or margarine. In the other, sauté some diced onions in similar shortening until they're soft but not brown. A volume about half that of the livers is appropriate. When the onions are ready, put them in with the meat. Stir both together gently, not breaking up the livers, and cook a minute or so longer. Serve over hot buttered toast.

The Peacemaker was thirteen and one-half feet long, nearly four feet wide amidships and flat bottomed, with a camber to it to make it ride better.

"Will it be big enough?" I asked doubtfully. "That water looks pretty rough."

"It'll ride like a cork," Charlie Ohland assured me. Behind the seamed granite of his face, I could see experience and dreams combatting lifelong native caution. Like Kay, he had an intriguing foreign voice with only the pleasant trace of an accent. "I've noticed that the channel in here gets pretty shallow at times. You wouldn't be able to get through with too much of a draft."

Quentin Franklin Gething, called by the sourdoughs and Indians the *King of the River*, echoed my doubts one damp dusk, full of sweet spring smells, when he stopped by to eat with us.

"Looks pretty light and small," decreed our friend King, "but it's certainly substantial. It should do for you two if you take it easy. You'll want plenty of power to get up the canyon. No one ever shot it all the way, as you know, but you should be able to get up as far as the old mine."

"How big an outboard motor should we buy?" Brad asked.

"For its weight, I'd want at least a ten horsepower kicker," King said. "I can pick up one for you wholesale if you want."

"Wonderful, thanks," Brad said. "Will you, then? I'll write you out a draft on the Bay for the money."

"I'll get out the order in the next mail," King promised. "It should be arriving with Les Bazeley about the time the river has tamed down enough to navigate."

With typical old-world prudence, Charlie Ohland added oarlocks. It was while he was carving wide dry spruce oars, that in a pinch could be used like paddles, that the cliff swallows returned to their great colonies of gourdlike nests in the river cliffs. I could see the flash of their bright feathers as they turned in their swooping flight low above the water under the ledge, in whose still shadows was the reflection of each tree. Charlie also gave us a long pole, with a forged iron tip, that had drifted downriver one time.

Charlie and Bushman got along well from the start and the Irish wolfhound got into the habit of going to meet him mornings. One forenoon Charlie burst into our yard, ruddy faced and panting.

"Gun," he yelled at Brad, "gun! The dog has treed a bear and I don't know how much longer it's going to stay up there."

Bushman was circling the base of a tall spruce and barking wildly as the three of us ran down the trail. Charlie glanced at him and then upward. Following the line of his gaze, I saw a big furry shape half-clambering, half-sliding down the trunk.

"Give him one!" Charlie was shouting.

Even as he spoke, the bear loosened his grip and slipped the remaining few feet to the ground with rasping claws. Then he turned toward Bushman, grunting. At first, Brad told me later, his telescopic sight was filled with black fur. Then the animal towered upward on his short hind legs and Brad saw the white patch that marked the bear's throat. He was close enough to hold on that as he squeezed the trigger. The bear reared backward, standing even higher.

"Give him another one," Charlie yelled. "Another one before . . . ."

The blast of the second shot drowned his words. The beast lurched sideways, tottered, then crumbled. My ears were ringing and I was breathing hard. I just stood there while Bushman ran in close, snapping.

Brad and Charlie started dressing and skinning the bear which, although brown furred, was a black. My husband told me, "If you don't mind bringing both saddled horses, Charlie and I can take half of this fellow back to the cabin and you can ride the other half to Kay in town. Do you want the fur, Charlie? It's still nice and sleek."

"I haven't any room for it, thanks," Charlie Ohland said, pausing to take a carborundum sharpening stone out of his pocket.

"Then we've got just the place for it at the head of our bunk," Brad said. "Get away from there, Bush."

"He thinks he did it all by himself," I said.

"He did, pretty much," Charlie said. "Thanks to him, we're in for some fine eating."

"I should be back home in time to get on a mulligan for tonight," I promised. "We can have liver this noon."

When Brad was writing *Living Off The Country*, he and I tasted every kind of wild meat we could come by handily—wolf, lynx, cougar, bison, muskrat, coyote, beaver, crow and so on, together with moose, caribou, elk, antelope, mountain sheep and goat. We also sampled opinions. Those who dine on bear meat fairly often, we found, are almost unanimously agreed that the North American wilderness affords no more delicious game, with the single exception of mountain sheep—and the last is only the best meat, wild or tame, I've ever eaten anywhere.

Many hunters, most of whom have never tasted bear meat nor smelled it cooking, are prejudiced against the carnivore as food for one reason or another. One reason often heard concerns the animal's eating habits. Yet the most ravenous bear is a finicky diner when compared to such delicacies as chicken and lobster.

It's true enough that not even a plump young yearling furnishes good steaks, which is where many culinary attempts end. The meat is too stringy and it has to be fried or broiled very long to avert any danger from trichinosis. But even an oldster big enough to carpet a cabin will cook up into roasts so moist and savory that you have to eat them to believe them. The meat then so resembles top-grade beef that you can serve it as such to individuals who've vowed they'd never touch bear meat and actually have them coming back for second and third helpings. I've seen more than one convert made that way.

And the mulligans? Well, if bear weren't such good eating, Brad would have given up hunting them after collecting our first two or three.

In the fall any excess fat should be trimmed off before the meat is cooked. This fat should then be heated in open pans to extract the grease. Strained into jars, that of the black bear hardens into a clear white solid that makes the best shortening that any user I've talked to has ever come across. That procured from a grizzly is also excellent and, when similarly rendered, remains a more easily measured oil. Both are also prized in the farther places for everything from medicine to mixing with molasses for Yankee butter.

The bear hide, tacked fleshed-side out on the south cache wall, had just started to dry when The Peacemaker was done. The outboard motor arrived soon afterward and Ted brought it up to us, along with some supplies, in his wagon. Dust caught up by the iron rims of the wagon wheels trailed yards behind on a light downriver breeze that was alive with the frail fragrance of popping poplar buds.

But the Peace River had swelled with the spring melt in the mountains. Now, mingled with the still jumping procession of ice cakes came silt, brush, broken limbs and entire great trees: cumbersome roots twisted and dipped in such slow motion that they seemed to be challenging us to climb aboard. The racing torrent was a never-ending scenario these early May days. I found myself tarrying by the hour in the golden sunshine in front of the cabin, enticed by the possibilities of what each succeeding second might bring. Even the sounds were as dramatic as gongs and trumpets swelling on a veering gale.

"There'll be a stage of water after most of this clears," King said, "when you'll be able to travel the side all the way to Les Allard's and Dad's old coal mine halfway up the canyon. But it has to be just the right flood tide. When there's too little water, you'll shear a pin traveling so close to shore and the middle of the river will still be too turbulent to tackle."

There was a point of land about 150 yards upriver from the cabin, where limestone cliffs gave away to shale, and behind this the current stilled while gathering itself to hurl across the ledge. We moored The Peacemaker in the placidity and waited for that magic day.

I'd had no experience with boats except for a little rowing on a lake an hour outside of Boston. But Brad had regularly canoed the racing wild Half Moon of the Southwest Miramichi River in New Brunswick, while still an advertising and newspaper man in Boston, before we finally took to the woods. He'd had no experience with outboard motors, though.

"But in a pinch," he told me, "we can use those oars like paddles and make do like a canoe, downstream anyway. And it'll pole up the current."

We couldn't keep ourselves off the river for long, especially not after Brad had bought us each a buoyant, orange-colored lifejacket. We didn't risk taking Bushman, though. At first, carefully following the north shore, we crept no further than Box Canyon; in the stillness there we took turns running the kicker.

Then, emboldened, we picked one serene day and made it all

the way to the Allard-Gething mine, on the river about eleven miles up the never fully navigated Rocky Mountain Canyon. We were a few yards above the point where Sir Alexander Mackenzie, the first explorer to cross the North American continent north of Mexico, had had to portage his freight canoe. There Brad sheared the last pin we had with us. We tied the boat to a rock by a dinosaur track and walked along the bank down to the cabin.

It was two weeks before we could get back: in that time, the character of the Peace had changed considerably. After shearing one pin because we'd hugged the shore too closely, Brad stationed me in the bow with an oar to look for rocks. Then when we circled a now-protruding ledge, a second pin sheared and the current caught us before we could get back near the bank.

Water boiled up in a fury of white air bubbles. The little suction holes twirled like dervishes. Behind me, Brad dug energetic holes in the stream with his own glistening oar, held like a paddle. The rush of water hurtled us on to leap into space over a part-cataract, then to weave in a controlled plunge through broken rapids.

"We can't get back now and I haven't time to put in another pin," Brad called to me in what I guess he hoped was a reassuring voice and, strangely enough, was. "Hold tight, Vena. I'll keep us straight with this paddle."

The current in midriver was suddenly quickening, gripping us turbulently. Brad dipped his blade to steady us. Then he was paddling furiously.

The day darkened. The rock walls were very narrow and white tumbling water filled what space there was between them. The peaceful water of two weeks before was gone. Inconsequentially, I noticed the tawniness of a streak of yellow ochre. Brad held the boat to the middle of the channel. It was exciting, intense, an exhilarating breath away from the rim of terror.

The narrow chasm between the overhanging precipices here, with claustrophobic suddenness, bothered me most. I tensed for a moment, the blade angled between my knees. I gripped the sides of the small craft with all my strength in an effort to stall the stifling panic into which I was threatening to catapult.

"Watch out for that sweeper!" Brad's warning was almost drowned by the roar of the water.

We were hurtling toward a giant basin, like the crater of a cold volcano, that sloped precipitously toward the tree-fringed skyline. A huge eddy whirled here. Half-inundated, a huge dead spruce clawed at us from where the current had wedged it among the rocks.

The light was still dim. I was half-blinded as well by the wind-hurtled spray, but I started paddling again, too. I watched the half-drowned tree leap at us but now, because of our joint efforts, the boat was on the crest of the water. Then it fell off again. The fringes of the whirlpool quickened about the plywood sides, but the craft was clear.

The now smooth green surface raced on, faster than I had believed even this part of the Peace River could run. The glassy surface began to break before little ripples. The ripples grew into washboard waves. Suddenly before us was the churned flurry of more rapids and their steady, deafening roar.

The river tilted and made its charging, exalting drop through a whitely jagged cataclysm. We strove to keep in the middle of this racing tumult, pulling hard. The boat pitched forward, bucked aloft, and the dark, ochre-stained cliffs streaked past us.

A tingle of excitement quickened my reactions. I found myself cooperating in meeting every fresh challenge keenly, alertly. There was no room, I knew, for even one mistake. Lifejackets or not, it Brad and I should overturn in this icy cold torrent, only a miracle could save us from dying from exposure.

The righthand shore was near, all awash to the cliff face. We went through a dark glitter of spray, as Brad propelled us from the bank's danger. He yelled at me.

"Bail!"

Water poured aboard for an instant, while the boat dropped as though the bottom of the river had disappeared from beneath us. I had my knees braced against the sides, but the drop and rise jolted me forward. It didn't affect my balance, though, and after the great jar I managed to wedge my oar in the prow and grab the large, floating tea pail.

"I can't keep up," I shouted back, bailing furiously.

"Do your best."

I wondered if a side had been punctured or if all that water was coming in over the gunwales. Glancing back, I saw Brad shove his paddle deep to straighten us. The craft bounced and swayed toward the head of more rapids, toward one huge boulder against which the current struck and broke into spray. Then we were past that and among smaller, darkly awash obstacles. The river charged, and leaped, and threw up cold layers of drops. Nowhere could I see a safe channel.

"Rocks," I shouted.

Brad decided to stay in the middle, fighting to keep steerage in the maelstrom. The vicious water tossed the bow into the air, with me holding on again for moments with both hands, then worried it as it careened back. Long curling waves rolled aboard, first on one side and then on the other, until it seemed as if we were going to be flooded if not actually upset.

Something scraped the bottom of the boat, half-buckling the rib beneath my knees. Brad still maintained control although his every tendon, too, must be aching. But it was as if only our last remaining buoyancy were resisting the roiling, downward pull. The boat wallowed heavily, although I was once again bailing with all my strength.

The next instant it shuddered with unnatural ponderousness. The rushing reefs, sheer and jagged, blurred on either side.

"That last rock got us," I yelled. "We'd better get ashore and bail out."

"Where," Brad gasped, "do you suggest?"

Cross currents, sloshing aboard, increased our unwieldiness. Frantically, Brad shoved his oar deep to steady us. Creaking, veering dizzily, the thirteen-footer reeled on. Brad, clothes plastered to his lankiness by the icy wind, had to exert every muscle to prevent us from turning broadside in the current and capsizing. I could see the sun on the top of the cliffs, but here everything was misty gray shadow through which the river danced whitely.

We plunged on in wheeling, drunken lunges. The constant swerving and the steady shock of dropping and then being tossed up again almost dizzied me. Even in quiet water now, I knew, there would have been a curious feeling of instability to the waterlogged craft despite all we could do to maneuver it.

Here it was as if each roll and chop were a fear-maddened, foam-maned horse, kicking at us as we passed. The boat sloshed, creaked, and wallowed unsteadily. Again water drove aboard, apparently from every direction at once.

"We're going over," I yelled.

"If we do, go through the rapids feet first and make for shore as soon as you can."

It seemed as if the last had come. Up, up we floundered. The bow—with me a disconsolate figure in it, wondering if I were ever going to get a breathing space again—hovered uncertainly over a yawning gulf. Glancing over my shoulder as I bailed, I could see Brad holding us, with tired muscles, from tilting. We poised an instant, the beleaguered stern nearly at a level with the water that boiled in a threatening eddy, sucking water into pirouetting holes an inch in depth.

Applying all his strength to the paddle, Brad somehow managed to hold upright. Giddily, we dipped over and hurtled abruptly downward. Spume assailed us from every side. My heart seemed to stop hammering.

Then, swamped and nearly capsized, we wallowed into the quiet wideness of the river, below the last rapids above our cabin. Wet and bedraggled though I was, I felt ten feet tall.

"We'll live forever!" Brad was shouting.

13

Spring Peepers

"Brad, you made it," I cried jubilantly.

"Yes, only it was we," Brad said emphatically. "We'd have sunk halfway through if it hadn't been for your paddling and your bailing."

After carrying the heavy outboard motor up on dry shale, he turned back to examine the boat. Its bow was grounded on the steeply sloping bank and safely tied to a birch.

"Is it all right?" I asked anxiously.

"I can't see yet, Vena. It's too full of water."

He found the blackened tea pail floating in the bow where I had been bailing. Standing by the stern in ankle-deep water, he started to scoop canfuls of river from the craft. I wondered grimly how much of the water had come in over the gunwales and how much was due to leakage.

Luckily, the boat was in pretty good shape.

"Two new ribs and another double sheet of marine plywood up in the bottom of the bow, and it'll be as good as new," Brad exulted. "I'll have it fixed in no time. But there's no hurry. After this, we stay off the river until the current moderates."

"How long will that be?" I wanted to know.

"To be absolutely safe," Brad said, "about a month, judging from past years. The cabin is just around the corner. Do you want to sit in the bow and fend us off the rocks with an oar while I pull us there? I may as well set in the kicker, too."

I could hear Bushman's deep barking from where he was chained to a birch in front of the cabin.

"Bush knows we're back," I said. "As soon as we get this up on the ledge, I'll go and turn him loose. I wonder if we'll ever be able to take him with us?"

"He should be all right as soon as the current quiets," Brad said. "At least, he won't give any trouble about jumping overboard. Judging from him, I guess Irish wolfhounds don't much like getting wet. Speaking of that, we'd better get up and change. Are you as hungry as I am?"

"I left a bear mulligan simmering on the back of the stove," I said.

"Mmmmm," he said with a grin. "Dumplings?"

"They'll only take about a dozen minutes after I get them mixed," I promised.

"That's for us, then," he said. "Ready to shove off?"

"I'm ready."

"This will only take a few minutes. Then we can put rollers under the boat and haul it, high and dry, right up on the ledge where I can work on it."

It was really spring. That afternoon when we were on the flat behind the cabin gathering wild greens, spring peepers seemed to be all around us, calling with such a shrill clatter that it sounded similar to a wagon whose axles needed greasing. When I finally found one of these little frogs, I realized why they were so hard to see. They were only about an inch long and the color of the dead cottonwood leaves that had survived from fall.

"Where have they been all winter?" I asked Brad.

"They just dig into the mud of this marsh when the days start to get too cold for them," he said. "They hibernate there until the weather is up around fifty degrees again."

"Like bear and chipmunks?" I asked.

"Sort of," he said, "except that not even the black bears really hibernate. They just sleep a lot. Their body temperatures only fall a few degrees, and they can be awakened rather easily—not like a woodchuck, whose temperature drops below forty degrees. Instead of breathing half a dozen times a minute, a woodchuck takes a breath only every five minutes and has a heartbeat only every several minutes. These little tree frogs are really cold-blooded creatures that hibernate until the warm weather returns, then awaken, hungry and ready to mate. Those're their mating calls."

"Oh," I said and then asked, "Suppose the weather turns cold again?"

"Then they'll just dig down into the mud once more until it warms up," he said. "Do you have a bag handy?"

"Yes, here you are."

"Thanks," he said. "Here's a nice patch of lamb's quarters."

But I was still thinking of the frogs, which had so interested Thoreau:

In almost all climes the tortoise and the frogs are among the precursors and heralds of this season, and birds fly with song and glancing plumage, and plants spring and bloom, and winds blow, to correct this slight oscillation of the poles and preserve the equilibrium of nature. As every season seems best to us in its turn, so the coming in of Spring is like the creation of Cosmos out of Chaos and the realization of the Golden Age.

A single gentle rain makes the grass many shades greener. So our prospects brighten on the influx of better thoughts. We should be blessed if we lived in the present always, and took advantage of every accident that befell us, like the grass which confesses the influence of the slightest dew that falls on it; and did not spend our time in atoning for the neglect of past opportunities, which we call doing our duty. We loiter in winter while it is already spring.

below: Gathering snow to melt for soft-water washing. Brad split the wood and I stacked. During cold spells we burned more than a cord a week.

Chinook, all-round riding mare, with a light tarp, sleeping bag, extra wool shirt, and grub for a week behind the cantle of her saddle.

Roaring Peace River rapids in front of the second cabin.

Well, here in the wilderness Brad and I didn't make that mistake, I thought later that evening when we were dining on lamb's quarter, watercress and miner's lettuce along with our bear roast.

Because lamb's quarter has no harsh flavors, many deem it the best of the wild greens. A characteristic is that the grayish-green or bluish-green leaves have a floury, white, water-repellent mealiness, particularly on their under portions. I knew from other years that later in the season, red-streaks would appear on the stalks of the older plants. The more or less diamond-shaped leaves are like egg-shaped parallelograms with oblique angles, those on top being formed more like lanceheads with broadly toothed edges. Growing from one to four inches long, their general overall shape has given this wild edible its scientific name *Chenopodium*, which is Greek for goosefoot.

This wild spinach, a branching annual growing from one to about six feet high, was widely used as a green, both raw and cooked, by the North American Indians. It grows throughout the United States and Canada, from Alaska to Labrador and southward. It is found, Brad told me, mainly where the soil has been disturbed: in old gardens and yards, once-ploughed meadows, ditches, and along fences and roadsides. The entire young plant is edible, whereas from the older one, quantities of tender small leaves can generally be stripped.

"Uummm," I savored, sampling one now, "these are just right for salad."

"Let's not pick too many," Brad said. "I like the cereal we can make from them later by boiling the whole seeds until they're soft."

Lamb's quarter, sometimes called pigweed, has been found to contain 309 milligrams of calcium per 100 grams of the raw edible portions and 258 milligrams after this same amount has been boiled and drained. This percentage is all the more remarkable when you consider that the green is roughly 80 to 90 percent water. The same portion boasts 11,600 international units of vitamin A when raw and 9,700 when cooked, plus significant amounts of thiamine, riboflavin and niacin.

"Who needs vitamin pills here in the bush?" I asked now. "Well, I wonder what we'll find next?"

"There used to be some miner's lettuce down the trail near the brook," Brad said. "Interesting how it got its name."

When the Forty-Niners stampeded through California with

their gold pans and rockers, the scarcity of fresh food brought scurvy and allied infections into some of what are now ghost towns. The Indians and the Spanish taught many of the argonauts how to beat these vitamin-deficiency troubles, showing them the antiscorbutic plant that thus took on the name of miner's lettuce. Those prospectors who didn't relish salads, or who gathered the plant so long after spring that it was tough, settled for boiling it— ideally, in a very small amount of water until just tender. But we had no such difficulty today.

"More salad," I said when I first came upon a patch of this native green which grows profusely in shaded, moist situations from British Columbia across to North Dakota, down to California and Arizona. It has also spread to Europe and the Caribbean, where it's also eaten.

This member of the purslane family, scientifically known as *montia*, is easy to recognize. Several stems each, becoming some four to twelve inches long, lift from a cluster of basal leaves. The leaves, arising on long stems, vary in shape from slim and narrow to kidney-form or even roundish. Their greenness sometimes takes on a pale pinkish hue. The characteristic feature of miner's lettuce is that, usually about two thirds of the way up each stem, a pair of round leaves grow together to form a sort of cup, through whose middle the stalk continues.

Above these disks of leaves, the stalks develop an elongated flower cluster: each blossom has its own short stem and the whole matures from the bottom upward. The flowers are small, white or pinkish, and nodding, each usually with five petals and two sepals. They develop into shiny black seeds that are sought by quail, doves, buntings, finches, grosbeaks, juncos, large siskins, sparrows and towhees. A number of mammals, including our horses, eat the leaves.

"Now that we're here, we may as well round out your salad with some watercress," Brad said. "At least, no one lives anywhere along this brook yet, so we don't have to worry about contamination. Be sure to leave the roots, Vena."

"I always do," I said, "except for that handful I got a couple of years ago so we could try steeping them for tea."

"It was good, too," Brad remembered.

"I just covered each teaspoonful with a cup of boiling water and let it steep for five minutes."

You're probably familiar with watercress, since this member of the mustard family, scientifically known as *cruciferae*, is common throughout Canada and the States. It grows in every state and, indeed, throughout the world, but is especially profuse in this Northern Hemisphere. Pungently tasty either cooked or in its native state, it is generally preferred raw. However, I've found that the briefly simmered leaves, stems, flowers and young pods are not only hard to beat among the boiled greens, but a handful adds zest to most other edible greens.

A tangy and interesting supplement to any salad, watercress is also a prime appetizer and will enliven hors d'oeuvres. Enjoy its characteristic peppery flavor in sandwiches, too, where it has been relished as long as these food snacks have been known.

Watercress, too, is easily recognizable. The usually prostrate and often floating plant thrives in cold water and wet places, growing in mats or clumps. It is characterized by innumerable little white, threadlike roots. The roots are tough and should in the main be left, in any event, so that the cress can continue to spread.

The minute white flowers, appearing from May to August depending on geographic location, are usually inconspicuous. Arranged in mustardlike crosses, many of the flowers extend from the stem joints; all blossom on a succession of tiny stocks attached to a longish stalk. The cross we gathered had tiny blossoms. They'd later develop needlelike pods from about one half to one inch long which, if still tender to the bite, would be tasty, too. Dense green leaves, dark and shiny, with smooth but wavy edges, grow with three to eleven smooth and roundish segments, the biggest of which is at the end.

We could have gathered more wild edibles. Fireweed, for example, was already beginning to sprout. But we had enough.

Strolling back toward the cabin hand in hand with Brad, I remembered what Justice William O. Douglas had said:

Only when there is a wilderness can man harmonize his inner being with the wavelengths of the earth. When the earth, its products, its creatures, become his concern, man is caught up in a cause greater than his own life and more meaningful. Only when man loses himself in an endeavor of that magnitude does he walk and live with humility and reverence.

14

A Walk at Night

The golden spring days ambled by, then the weeks and months and finally the years, until Hudson Hope became crowded with more and more people and houses and trailers. Heavy earth-moving machinery clanged in, some bulldozing an airstrip along the north side of the portage road where an occasional jet now landed. It became spring once more.

Brad and I, with Dhulart dun Delgan (Bushman's registered name), had been in town for the mail and now we were heading home. We passed the pioneer-built log church. Its graceful steeple, brown against the blue of the Peace River on whose high north bank the church stood, suggested in the dusk the thresh of an angel's wings. A single silver gleam of lamplight fanned from the Gethings' kitchen window, making the last lingering twilight deeper and more fascinatingly blue. Somewhere, what seemed to be a small dog barked. Bushman ignored it, scampering along with our mail and our library books—postage paid both ways—in his packsack.

I smelled pine smoke and heard a low-geared truck, perhaps with a load of high-grade soft coal from King Gething's mine on Bullhead, backfiring down the road that zigzagged from the portage to the flat below. All this was against the low, murmuring, almost purring sound that the Peace River made at night. It flowed past a great, gushing spring on the slope just north of the now-closed H.B.C. compound. The spring was perhaps a remnant of a calmer river. The original river, later clogged with moraine, had flowed where the shorter portage road now cuts to the head of Rocky Mountain Canyon. The site of the spring was the reason for Hudson Hope being built here, a log cabin at a time.

"It's changing," Brad said disconsolately, nodding at what had been a baseball field and was now filled with trailers.

Hudson Hope; the helicopters in what had been the H.B.C. garden where, under the urging of twenty hours of daily sunshine, Dave and Marian Cuthill's summer vegetables had grown to record sizes; the trailers and other evidences of the coming dam; encroaching outriders of civilization: the whole man-made world disappeared behind us as we walked along the winding trail toward the glen and the ledge and our present cabin.

Then the last vestiges of the village were gone. Dudley Shaw's new little cabin in a clump of poplars toward the river bank had vanished behind us, along with a fenced field of oats. For two miles there were only the medicinal-smelling poplars and the fireweed and the river—now a faint, cliff-patterned glass of entrenched shadows that sucked luster from a moon-silvering sky where the Aurora Borealis whipped like a breeze-undulated scarf. All the rest of civilized Canada was gone: remote, improbable and now scarcely recalled beyond the sheer, dim cutbanks.

Brad had a light, carrying step. He swung along so that his moccasined feet barely cleared the ground, setting them down as straight and sure as an Indian. I found I was falling behind.

"Sorry, Vena," he apologized when he heard me behind him in the cool forest aisle, trying to catch up. "There's no hurry. Guess I was just thinking."

"At least," I said, "it's still the same here."

"For awhile, anyway," he said. "While you and Vesta were having tea, King and Larry were telling me that Alwin Holland, the former schoolmaster and surveyor here, plans to give the glen next to us to the town for a public park."

"At least, that'd mean they'd have to put in a good road to our gate," I said.

"Aren't there already enough roads?" Brad asked.

I thought that over. Where there are plenty of roads, life drains out of a city at night and is confined in the big lit-up apartment houses. But the nighttime forest lanes come alive as wild creatures, too timid to stir during the day, venture into the sheltering blackness.

Where a spread of spruce grew thick, the trail at our feet became invisible and we kept on it both by feel and by glancing upward through the dim slit in the trees. To the north, chatoyant green ribbons of light streamed out of ebony nothingness: they shimmered high above the budded, creaking trees in whose limbs the birds would soon be teaming together in their first dawn twittering, then streaked out of sight with abrupt, tumultuous verdancy into the jet emptiness.

Behind us in the east, the first edge of what I knew was a nearly full moon appeared, illuminating the snow patches that still remained on the hillsides in such a way that the land seemed dressed in white lace. Springtime had arrived with such a bound this year that pussy willows were still flowering on their red wands. Arnica daisies (some of which I was drying before soaking them in alcohol to manufacture liniment) were making their yellow rush. Soon moonlight was blooming and blossoming over the entire countryside.

"Warm enough?" Brad asked.

"Nice and cozy," I said.

We were walking side by side, his long fingers entwined with mine.

As we proceeded along the winding trail, I knew when to expect every bend and every straight, unimpeded stretch, every glade and toppled forest giant and muddy spot with its animal tracks, as vividly as if we had been coming that unchanged way a dozen years.

"Why," I thought aloud, "so we have."

"Have what?" Brad asked.

"We've been walking and riding this trail for a dozen years," I said.

I thought of Boston's Esplanade and New York's Central Park, which both would have been sinister this time of day and where—the shadows like forms in ambush and the moon only a meek lamp against what lurked in the night—I wouldn't have dared to walk without a handgun permit.

My nostrils caught the night smell of the river, humid with the returning spring warmth, refreshing and vigorous. I detected the reawakening redolence of lodgepole pine and an occasional suggestion of distant woodsmoke, perhaps from some settler's or Indian's land-clearing fire.

For about a mile and a half the trail, wide enough only for a rattling wagon or a creaking sleigh, wound along the high north rim of the Peace River. Halfway down its looming northern foothills was many a favorite lookout bed of moose. Then the Peace dropped down an incline to the remains of an old channel, called the glen, where for the first time since Hudson Hope the bank again met the shore.

Here we emerged into the open again, by the pole corral and our nickering horses with our fenced clearing beyond. Blended into the gentle slope up which we carried our water, I glimpsed ahead of me the low comfortable angles and the wide roof of our second wilderness home. Something in the fragile calm kept us from speaking until we reached our gate.

"I'll water and feed the cayuses if you want to get supper started," Brad suggested then.

"Down," I said to the anxious wolfhound. "Come on, Bush, and I'll get that pack off you and fix your supper. How about the last of our moose steaks tonight?"

"Fine with me," Brad agreed. "I'll dig them out of the snow for you on the way in."

My thoughts dwelled on the woods and the log cabin. They gave us more than time, but it was the luxury of leisure that made the very air feel different. And I had a sense of being different, inhaling that air: relaxed, unhurried, still contemplative but with any edge of sadness removed from it.

High above, a plane thrummed through the moonlight, its red lights blinking off and on.

"I suppose we'll be seeing more and more of those," Brad said.

But I was looking at the blackness among the stars, that emptiness in time where the tiny gleam of our own past days scatters for all ages without a sign, bearing the totality of our yesterdays with it.

The mail had contained a grant from the National Wildlife Federation in Washington, D.C., to research and write a first-hand, detailed book on living off the country, to be entitled *Survival With Style*. Brad stayed home the next morning to start outlining it.

Saddling Cloud, then letting the gelding pick his own pace, I rode slowly from the Peace River up the Block Line to the flat that was already alive with thousands of raspberry blossoms. There I turned left up the old riverside trail which Dudley had kept open as part of his winter trapline. I passed some of the tallest poplar and spruce in the country where a half-swamp watered their roots, traversed a squirrel-chattering evergreen grove by a spring on the western flank of our property, and sloshed across a quick little stream.

Emerging on a sharply eroded incline to higher land, after the gray had had his drink, I continued for a short distance through berry-bush-filled brule. Dudley had once set a back fire here to thwart one of the springtime blazes that the local Cree and Beaver Indians often set to open the land for young food that brings in game; settlers also set them to clear grazing opennesses for their small cattle herds. I followed the path until it led once more to the high river bank.

There I dismounted, leaving the reins dangling so that Cloud could seek the slim green tidbits of False Soloman's Seal, whose ripened berries would later be as refreshing to me as cherry pop. Bushman joined me, coiling nearby as I dropped onto the yielding cleanness of a sprawl of juniper. I popped several of its ginlike blue berries into my mouth. Closing my eyes, I listened to the relaxing chatter of the rapids below and the rusty cawing of crows. I felt the spring sunshine delving, warm and persuasive, into every muscle of my body.

Maybe a half hour had gone gently past when I heard an entirely unexpected clattering and rumbling, and a half-track appeared. It stopped beside me; two men in open-throated khaki shirts, with tight khaki trousers stagged above heavy leather boots, got out and looked at me.

"Here, Bushman," I said. When he came to me, I grasped his chain collar.

"Good morning," said the older man, who had pale brown eyes and sunken black-stubbed cheeks. His veined, bony right hand was still white beneath its tan on the wheel.

"Good morning," I said.

"Is this the trail to Site One?" asked the second man, his plump face all the rounder with a smile, which he narrowed now around the stem of a low-bowled pipe. "The spot for the smaller power dam, that is."

"I know," I said. "It's on our original home site."

"This is the only trail we could find," the driver said.

"It's all we've ever had," I told him.

"It's going to take a lot of work," the round-faced man said. "I thought we were off it several times."

"No, you're headed right," I said, getting to my feet. Cloud, I saw, had worked several yards into the bush and was out of the way. "It's another two miles. Is the . . . the work going to start soon?"

"The big dam at the head of the canyon is going in first," the driver said. "Right now, here, we're getting ready to bring in a drilling crew so that we can see about the footing. That must be your present cabin back there by the islands. Well, we'll be staying up on the flat, so we shouldn't disturb you any. You'll get a good all-weather road out of it."

"And traffic," I added.

"Traffic?" the driver repeated.

The younger man prodded at the contents of his pipe with a penknife and grinned apologetically.

"Progress," he explained. "Land values are already going up. Your place, being in the middle, will be worth a lot more money. Well, good day and thank you. That's a fine looking dog you have."

"Glorious weather," the driver said, swinging back up into the vehicle and stepping on the starter.

The fumes seemed to be dimming the sunlight as they crashed away. I felt suddenly chilly. Then I saw that a cloud was wisping across the sun.

15

Journey to Where?

At dawn the eastern horizon was clear, brittle sharp against the blue intensity of the Peace River. A west wind was pulling at the loose oat strands in the mound of horse food, just persuasively enough to rustle them. The faint glow of the still-hidden sun turned the water, when it rushed around the edge of the ledge in front of the cabin, the color of a wild rose. A gray Canada jay swooped over it, solitary and silent.

We put halters on our horses and led them down the glen path to drink. Bushman loped ahead and paused only to bark at a red squirrel who, scampering to safety, perched on a spruce bough just above his head and scolded us all indiscriminately. I wondered again at the wisdom of spiders whose dew-clasping silver webs on the morning grass prognosticated another fair day.

"What say we take the boat and go across river?" Brad said. "At least, they haven't disturbed there yet."

"King Gething was telling me that there's talk about putting a bridge across the Peace by those ledges a half mile below our former home site," I said.

"Yes, I heard that, too." His words had a sharp, hard ring. "Then they can have a station at Chetwynd on that railroad the government is pushing along the Hart Highway from Prince George. A road from there to here, past Moberly Lake, will be a whole lot nearer for the dam supplies."

"It'll seem strange to have a bridge. Before, the only way to drive across the river, except on the ice, was on that Alaska Highway bridge between Fort St. John and Dawson Creek."

"I guess no one can stop what people call progress," Brad said. Then he smiled, thinly for him. "We'd better enjoy this wilderness as much as we can while we still have it."

"It seemed so remote, when we were considering it in Boston," I said, "on hardly any maps and only one human being for every twelve and a half square miles."

My voice had a hollow sound to it there between the narrow rock walls, where once the Gethings had brought coal on sleighs from the mine on the river in the middle of the canyon. Then I forced myself to smile, too.

"We can have a nice day," I said. "Let's climb to the top of that ridge a couple miles back. Would you rather have cheese or peanut butter and raspberry jam sandwiches?"

"Why not one of each?" Brad suggested. "They'll toast nicely and they'll taste good with our tea."

With Bushman lying cautiously in the bow and me seated in the middle, Brad turned the Peacemaker a hundred feet upriver, then crossed to the channel which raced along the north shores of the two central islands. He swerved between the lower of these—

the one on which the geese regularly nested—and Dudley's aptly named Teapot Island. Then, testing the depth of the water with a stick, he slowly moved to the mouth of the creek opposite the cabin, where he took two half hitches around a handy poplar with the bow line.

The sky was an intense blue by now and lofty cumulus clouds streamed lazily from northwest to southeast on a balmy breeze. I could hear a tractor working upriver, steadily and unrelentingly, although the pitch of its engine changed occasionally.

Looking at our rejuvenated cabin where it sat in the sunlight on the north bank, I wondered if *it* or I had changed the most since that first smokeless early February morning. Years before, Brad and I had ridden past it, while Dudley was still asleep inside, upon Ted Boynton's loaded sleigh on our way to what had become our first wilderness home. We'd had the entire world in the palms of our hands that morning. Maybe, I thought, we had both changed. Perhaps the fact was just something to accept, like a partridge on a pine tree or the smile of a lover.

We built our noon fire by a quick little brook which must have had its start nearby, for we were near the crest of the main ridge. Below, across the clean sea of azure air, our cabin now looked as inconsequential as a child's block on a rug the color of corroded copper.

Upriver to the left was the companionable bulk of Bullhead Mountain which we had climbed several years ago, before the new mapmakers started to call it Portage Mountain and to name the bulge across the road Bullhead instead. Halfway up its slope, seemingly almost close enough to touch, I could make out the scree incline: at its bottom was King's lone coal mine and the cool spring around which he had built his small camp of frame buildings and log cabins. The largest structure was the long cook shack which had been one of the surplus buildings the Americans left behind when they quit the Canadian portion of the Alaska Highway.

"Cheese first?" I asked Brad, who was cutting and trimming two forked green willows.

"Cheese, toasted just long enough to start it melting, will be fine," he said. He looked around him: "It's like a park in here, isn't it?"

The widely spaced poplars did give that aspect, I realized, and parks have always intrigued me. Have you ever noticed that in metropolises, they tend to mirror nationalistic inclinations? Paris, for example, proffers somehow pompous stage sets with vistas. Tokyo's parks, like its people, are neat as chignons. Singapore's, except for the grotesque and garish Tiger Balm Gardens, are tropical jungles only barely quelled. New York's Central Park has a tentativeness to it, as if some future city administration will consider the land too priceless to be left any longer to trees, lakes and muggers. After all, before we'd left Boston, hadn't the city fathers already been talking of violating the ancient Common with an underground garage? Only in London—and to a lesser degree in Cape Town and Victoria—do the parks, beneath their grime, remain imbued with a strange and tranquil chivalry, as if they continue significantly despite the tenements and the hotels because they remain part of the British reverie of rustic content.

Over the poplar coals that Brad raked to one side for cooking, the aged cheddar cheese melted from between our sandwiches and browned delectably. The peanut butter sandwiches, sweetened with raspberry jam I'd put up from berries behind the cabin, were delicious, too, there in the open air. We ate beneath a gigantic spruce whose top captured the sun, shattered it with its rustling needles, and laid it on the ground about us in a shiver of gold and green.

All the most exquisite things are transient and perishable, I thought as we sat and sipped hot black tea.

"More tea?" I asked Brad.

"Not right now, thanks," he said, setting down his cup and leaning back to rest his elbows on the flowering sphagnum moss.

I followed suit, first rolling my yellow, red and green plaid H.B.C. shirt into a pillow. The rounded mass of Bullhead drifted lazily through my lashes, then I shut my eyelids completely. They felt warm beneath the drift of shadows and sunlight. Then I had a compulsion to open them; when I did, I saw that Brad, propped up on one elbow, was staring at me.

"Is something the matter?" I asked.

"I was mostly thinking," he said. "I was wondering what was our real beginning, only I can't think back far enough. I guess it all started for me one day when I was three: I took the family dog and climbed through the woods, just across the street it so happened, to a wooded cliff. This was back in Massachusetts, in Beverly, and all that district has been fully developed for years. But then it was woods, and I can remember how I could see our house, and the new athletic field which then was away out in the country, and miniature toy shops along Cabot Street downtown. Just me and the dog, and the wind whistling through the trees, and the space below."

"Your folks must have been worried when they found you were gone," I said, "or didn't they ever find out?"

"They soon found out, all right." There seemed to be a tinge of sadness in his smile. "After that I had to promise never to go there alone again, because they said it was too dangerous for a little boy. He might fall or become lost. They weren't much on the woods."

"But as you grew older?" I asked.

"Well, there were the Ernest Thompson Seton and the Daniel Carter Beard books," he said. "And then when I was twelve, the Boy Scouts of Troop Two—which was the best troop in town and won more prizes at the annual Topsfield Fair than any other Scout troop. It was great, largely because of the scoutmaster, Johnny Lee, a former sailor who'd once gone on a treasure hunt to Cocos Island. He taught me how to tie a turk's head; you know, that ring knot I made for you to hold your scarf together."

"I still use it," I said. "It's a good knot."

"Then there were the years of prep school and college, Kimball Union Academy and Bates, in the never-quite-tamed open spaces of New Hampshire and Maine." He sat up and clasped his hands around his khakied knees. "After that, twice a year at the very least, I took canoe trips along the wild Half Moon of the upper Southwest Miramichi River in New Brunswick, where it's little more than a brawling brook, or the Grand Cascapedia River in the interior of the Gaspé Peninsula in Quebec."

These, he told me now, were the weeks he had escaped from the confines of teeming, street-twisting Boston, his show-business trade paper editing, and his advertising work. Gradually, season by season, the brick walls of his small Gloucester Street apartment swelled about him, until all the knowledge and the sadness, all the loveliness and the apprehension of the universe were hemmed in for him, relentlessly, inside their dull, intimate limits. His only consolation had been his best friends, Bill and Eleanor Otis—with stems back to the American Revolution—and their two little sons, Jocko and Billy.

Doubt had been there, too, along with the rest: in the pages of the Thoreau books; in the growing piles of outdoor clothing and tentage and other equipment; in tantalizing old flintlocks and percussion-cap rifles on the wall and the green-backed deerskins on the oak floor; in blackened railroad yards at the head of the street and the ceaseless Commonwealth Avenue automobiles, paced by yellow and green and red traffic lights; in the direction of the Esplanade and the Charles River, with Harvard and the Massachusetts Institute of Technology across its soiled waters.

Then I had come along and all that had changed. For Brad had never wanted to take to the woods alone, and he was older, and the years of hunting and fishing in Canada and Maine had taught him some of the ways of the wilderness, and he was ready.

"I know what you mean by doubt," I said, pushing the end of a dead branch further into the fire. "Only with me it was more like a terror."

"Terror?" he repeated, his eyes icy blue.

It took me a moment to think how to put it. When I answered him, my words seemed to me to be falling slowly and agonizingly.

"I knew there was some special reason you wanted me to meet you for lunch in that below-the-sidewalk cafe on Newbury Street," I said. "I was breathing so hard when I came down the steps that I could hardly keep up with myself. I wanted to run back so that I wouldn't have to know what it was you were going to say. But I had to know. Then, the next instant, I was walking downstairs again. I came over to where you were waiting, cool and collected, and all of a sudden I was breathing quietly, telling myself: yes, of course, whatever Brad wants, I'll go along with him."

Brad looked as if he were going to say something, but he pushed another branch further into the coals instead.

"Afterward it was like that, too," I continued, "when we were buying me clothes to take and all I could find that I liked, which were warm enough, were ski togs. We were more together than ever and I was glad we were together, and at the same time I was afraid. All that talk of the wilderness was so new to me."

"I thought the reason was that you didn't want to give up dancing. That you didn't want to stop producing musical shows, to quit the show business that had been your life since you were a little girl."

"Some of it was that, too." I looked up from where flames were licking the fresh fuel, to meet the intentness of his blue eyes. "Oh, you know . . . . It was my whole life's suddenly having purpose, suddenly going the way it had been destined from the first. And I was glad we were going away together; very, very glad, Brad. But all this while I was frightened, too, because the career I'd been making for myself was getting away. But I did know one thing for sure."

"What, Vena?"

"In a city, a man and a woman are not so close, Brad. There's always someone else in a city, someone to come in and clean, restaurants to feed you, someone else to go to a show with afterward. You don't have to depend on each other for everything, as you do here in the wilderness. Here I know you need me, just as much as I need you. Here we are one. I like it that way."

My words had been soft and controlled. Now, as I came to the last sentence, they faltered. I turned my eyes away and I felt my palms rubbing at them. Then Brad's arms were about me.

"Dear," he said.

I couldn't move nor answer. His grasp tightened. Briefly, I felt my body grow rigid. Then I began to shiver, and I had to speak, although I was afraid to trust my voice beyond a whisper.

"Let me lean against you, just for a minute," I murmured.

He held me as if I were something delicate, something fragile.

"Not like a child," I told him. "Like a wife."

16

The Atlin

The campfire had burned to ashes when I awoke. The late afternoon sun was warm and slanting, reaching us now through the bronze-trembling silver leaves of a huge poplar which was spattering us with shadows and shine. Bushman was coiled nearby and Brad lay quietly on the bed of sphagnum moss with his eyes shut, breathing with a long, even rhythm.

I was facing Brad, my head resting on his outflung arm. He was warm, his face a deep tan against the flower-flecked grayness of the moss: the same kind of moss I had gathered by the bagful to chink our cabin. If his lids were open, I knew, his eyes would be the same color as the intensely blue sky.

"Brad," I whispered gently.

He did not stir. I sat up, staying there for a few moments, studying him. Then I started to get things together for Bushman's pack: the stainless steel cups, a wad of unused Fort Garry Tea in its waxed-paper wedge, and the blackened tea pail which was only a large fruit-juice can with its top smoothly removed and a bail of copper wire looped through two tiny nail holes just below the rim.

Bushman came slowly to his feet, as if it were an effort, then his tail began flailing. It was as though he were a puppy again—stepping bravely, if uncertainly, from a now-open crate after a transcontinental journey—and Brad and I were children once more: the paths of the three of us already inexorably pointing toward this converging on a British Columbia mountainside above Hudson Hope.

I thought of all we had been talking about, how Dante had said that the bitterest of all pangs is to remember happier days. But somehow I wasn't unhappy although, while the river hadn't changed and the mountains hadn't changed and even Brad and I had not altered, yet everything was different.

"You're looking very serious, Vena," came Brad's low-pitched voice.

Then he, too, lifted himself into a sitting position. The arm that had been outstretched on the moss curved warmly around me and he covered my mouth with his.

When I could speak again, I said everything in a single burst. "I don't ever want to live in cities again, Brad!"

"We don't have to," he said, shaking his head slowly. "Neither do I."

"Suppose they make Hudson Hope into one? We saw that happen to Dawson Creek and Fort St. John."

"There are other wildernesses."

"Where, for us?"

"The Atlin maybe," he said, "over to the northwest."

I thought of a letter we had just answered, as we answer all our mail, feeling that when anyone takes the trouble to write, he certainly deserves the courtesy of a reply. In fact, I still had this one in my pocket, partly because on its back I'd jotted down Claire Barkley's recipe for highbush cranberry jelly. It said, in part:

For some years now I have been moved to reading whatever of your camping and wilderness survival books I can lay hands to, by something to which I am at a loss to put a name. It is an affinity for the out-of-doors which is not answered by any of my background or upbringing. There is more a core of emptiness within me which craves release in the ways of the wild country; something which is remote and yet holds the promise of wondrous fruition . . . just as the tree lies dormant during the chill winter months only to burst forth with life at the coming of Spring.

Recently, while reading At Home in the Woods, I came across where you quote Thoreau: "We need the tonic of wildness—to wade sometime in marshes where the bittern and the meadow hen lurk, and hear the booming of the snipe; to smell the whispering sedge where only some wilder and more solitary fowl builds her nest, and the mink crawls with its belly close to the ground."

Although I have been unable to sense these things in my 21 years, somehow I knew the deep feeling expressed within the passages; the quiet estimation of one who has known and loved them for what they are, and what their being reveals. At the same time I commenced reading On Your Own in the Wilderness and— perhaps due to that unrecognizable reaction to Thoreau's words—I became more and more engrossed with your book. With my next visit to the bookstore I picked up a copy of your informative book How To Live in the Woods on Pennies a Day.

The story of the break you and your husband made, told bit by bit, glimpse by glimpse, within the more apparent and important purpose of the book, drew that unexplained feeling from within me once more, and I became aware of the growing conviction that I would do my best to duplicate what you had already proven is not only possible but most desirable!

The only drawback, and a temporary one at that, is my present involvement with the Canadian Armed Forces, and my posting to the east coast with the Sea Element. While a check to my hopes and plans, my employment as a Hull Technician will train me in several trades which will prove useful in the woods. I have little

*over four more years to serve, but that time can best be spent
learning and putting that nest egg away.*

*Needless to say, your books on living in the wilderness have
aided tremendously in shaping my resolve. I am now firmly com-
mitted to making for the woods, most likely in northern British
Columbia. And, so, my thanks go to you and Brad for the en-
couragement and great help you have been to me. My only question is: will there be a wilderness to go to when I am ready?*

When we wrote back to him, we told him that maybe the Atlin
region of British Columbia would be what he's looking for.
Bounded on the north by the Yukon, on the west by Alaska's panhandle, and on the south and east mainly by the drainage of
streams flowing into the Arctic Ocean or the Pacific, are 42,750
square miles inhabited by only some 600 Indians and sourdoughs.
Enormous tracts are truly wilderness, have no permanent population, lack transportation and communication facilities, and have
been almost untouched by any form of industrial activity except
for small mines and some logging. This country is even more wild
than the regions west of the Alleghenies were to early American
pioneers. It's country you can grow in.

The Atlin has a rigorous but not severe climate. Pleasant and
fairly warm summers, with prolonged hours of daylight, give way
rather abruptly to stimulatingly cold winters. The forests of the
Coast Mountains and the larger coastal valleys, if you put up your
cabin that far west in the area, have high annual rates of
precipitation as well as more equable temperatures, but the interior is considerably drier. Twenty inches of moisture or less is
typical, except in the Cassiar Mountains, where up to thirty
inches is the rule.

Mining and prospecting are the principal activities, with a very
small amount of logging and sawmilling. Trapping and big-game
guiding round out the incomes of quite a few. It's a country where
a man is on his own.

Moose weighing nearly a ton, the largest caribou in British
Columbia, Stone and Dall sheep, the surprisingly tasty mountain
goat, grizzly, black bear, and a few blacktail deer will keep your
cache filled. A wide variety of upland birds liven the hunting
season. There are so many lake trout and whitefish that those not
used for human consumption are snapped up as food for the local
dogs. And while you're hunting and fishing, you can be looking

for your fortune in gold, silver, copper, lead, zinc, asbestos, coal, and widely sought strategic metals. With the prevailing prices on today's at-last-free markets, gold is worth the entire price of admission. George Sullivan's book, *The Modern Treasure Finder's Manual*, contains some excellent how-to material about gold prospecting and so does Brad's new *Looking for Gold*.

With civilization coming to Hudson Hope, if we were starting out all over again, the Atlin is where we'd head. Either there or to the golden Yukon!

There is still an abundance of wilderness.

Hudson Hope was not what it was when we saw it first: a sleepy little log cabin settlement of some thirty-five sourdoughs clustered about an active H.B.C. Trading Post. But for us, since our friends and our roots were here, it was still intrinsically wilderness. Most of the new people were sticking to the roads. Except in the winter, when snowmobiles were already ranging far, we could step into the untracked woods almost anywhere and never see another human from one year's end to another.

A major consideration in your choice of a site is likely to be its hunting and fishing merits, since the bulk of your food will probably come from the land itself. A fat moose, for instance, will on the average supply a pound of meat for every day in the year. If you are married, your mate can also buy the low-cost resident's license; so there are two moose. The same thing goes for the older children. Some of this meat you'll have to dry or can, of course, if you're going to make it last through the warm months. But your neighbors will show you how.

There are also myriad birds, from Canada geese to the grouse and ptarmigan; the small game that are legal the year around; predators such as lynx, whose fricasseed white meat looks and tastes like chicken; and odd delicacies such as beaver tails which many trappers will be glad to share with you. All Canadian and Alaskan birds, freshwater fish, and nearly every part of their animals are good to eat. An occasional exception is the liver of the polar bear and of the ringed and bearded seal, which become so excessively rich in vitamin A at certain times that, to be safe, they are just as well avoided by pets and man.

Food costs these days consume one third or more of the money the average family has to spend for living expenses. The largest single expenditure in nearly every instance is for meat, and no wonder. Sizzling steaks, succulent chops and juicy roasts are fine fare. As a matter of fact, rare fresh meat is the single food that contains every one of the nutritional ingredients necessary for rugged health. In other words, you can keep in peak condition on a diet of fresh, rare, fat meat and water alone for a month, a year, or a decade.

No one, obviously, wants to save money at the price of good health. It's a proved fact that the right food gives you more energy, sturdier health, tougher resistance, increased mental alertness, and a happier outlook. The right food can also keep you young longer, increasing life expectance while postponing old age. Scientists have proved that an individual well fed from childhood has a likelier chance to enjoy a long prime of life. But at any age, anyone is better off when he is better fed.

Most of us don't want to cut down on this ideal grub. If anything, we'd probably enjoy sitting down to more sirloins, porterhouses and barbequed spareribs. If you live in the woods, you have every opportunity of doing just this and for free. Brad's *Wilderness Cookery, Gourmet Cooking For Free*, and the *Home Book of Cooking Venison and Other Natural Meats* explain preparation and cooking.

What about the wild fruits and vegetables to go with those sputtering steaks, fat-marbled roasts and steaming mulligans? There are literally hundreds to choose from. Recognizing a dozen or so will do the trick, however. Every backwoodsman has a few favorites he'll point out to you. Others you know already: strawberries, dandelions, mustard, clover, fireweed and so on. For a really productive and happy time, though, I'd suggest you take along some reading matter on the subject. Brad's *Feasting Free on Wild Edibles* and his all-color *Field Guide to Edible Wild Plants* cover most of the usable plants that grow in the Canadian and Alaskan regions—where you'll likely be making your home—as well as those in the States where you may as well start making their happy acquaintance.

That takes care of most of your food. For the price of seeds and a minimum of tools, you can augment nature's bounty with the output of a small vegetable garden, enough to store in your cold cellar until the following spring. You can always keep a goat or cow to make your own cheese and yogurt for supplemental protein; eggs can be collected from birds' nests.

The initial move takes careful planning, partly because the selection of a wilderness niche is a highly individual matter. Much depends on what you want most and upon the compromises you are willing to make. Once you make the break, distances will be relatively unimportant. You'll be better advised to travel a couple of days farther, as a matter of fact, to get where you really want to be. That eventual store and post office, on the other hand, may as well be reasonably accessible.

Do you want moose for neighbors? How about tall open country where you can hunt and explore on horseback, where your saddle and pack animals can keep fat the year round on free graze? Or are you happiest in a canoe? What about setting up housekeeping in a ghost town?

Or try one of the immense regions scattered across the roof of the continent where, especially with gold soaring so in price, you'll have a reasonable chance of coming across a valuable mineral deposit while fishing, hunting, camping, exploring or just plain sauntering. What about free government schooling by mail? Free library books by mail, with even the return postage paid?

When your planning is done and you're ready to head back of beyond, you'll experience contentment and satisfaction different from anything you have ever known. The cost of a thing is the amount of life which has to be exchanged for it, immediately or in the long run. When the essentials are assured, there is an alternative to struggling for the luxuries. That's to savor life itself. What you're really buying, in other words, is time.

Once you and your duffle bags arrive at the jumping-off place, look around for a week or two. Often you'll come across a deserted prospector's or trapper's cabin which you can move into and fix up. Too, anyone can build a good log cabin from the ground up, as explained in our *How to Build Your Home in the Woods*, with nearly 150 on-the-spot drawings.

The job is not terribly difficult. It's far less complicated, for example, than putting up a satisfactory frame dwelling. Figure everything out on paper before you start. Then measure and mark. If you distrust your axmanship, use a saw instead.

When you return to visit civilization, what a tale you'll have to tell about this entirely different world of which you've become a part. Everyone who has sat by a crackling stove at night in a cabin deep in the wilderness wants to go back—everyone except people like Brad and me, that is. But that's because we're already here.

"We'd better be starting back." Brad's deep voice interrupted my reverie, and I saw that a string of cumulus clouds, like puffy exhalations of smoke, had moved across the western aster-blue sky and the lowering sun. Below, the azure of the ribboning Peace, embroidered by rapids and darkened even more by the steep cutbanks, had turned into a purple velvet band. We still had to cross it. "Come here, Bush, and get your pack. What in the world is he looking at?"

I followed the line of the dog's gaze along the bubbling dance of the little stream from which we had dipped our tea water. A hundred yards below, a small, thickset, slate-colored bird that I recognized as a water ouzel was walking along the streambed in its search for insects. Bushman, seemingly fascinated, did not move as the ouzel, with a bobbing motion that did not interrupt its stride, walked out of sight beneath the silvery current.

"Quite a sight, aren't they?" Brad said. The campfire seemed to be out, but when Brad tested a blackened chunk of wood with a boot, sparks flew up like stars. "Let me have the tea pail, honey, and I'll douse this down good."

As we started down the slope hand in hand, long shadows from a higher crag stretched over the conifers, stilling the squirrels. I was so silent and preoccupied, too, that it must have been a few moments before I was aware that Brad had stopped and, comforting me with an arm around my waist, stood close beside me. I managed a smile.

"Don't worry about the future, Vena," he said, pressing me gently against him.

"It's not just a matter of standing in a line at a supermarket or of thronging together at the latest play," I heard myself say, "but of thinking and feeling. It's not just what people believe and talk about, but what they really are."

My usually throaty voice sounded almost shrill to me and I was shivering. Brad didn't say anything for a moment; he just held me close. My quivering stilled against his strength and warmth, but he didn't let me go.

"I know what we really are, too," he said, lightly as the touch of a leaf. "We're not going to be caught by civilization again. Believe me, everything will be fine."

17

Starfish Creek

Through the years the sunny north bank of the Peace River where we lived hadn't changed, although from hour to hour, even minute to minute, it was different. Day and night followed one another, and sun and wind and rain. Now in the autumn, which had succeeded an ever more crowded spring and summer, snow and icy pellets of sleet made it always interestingly divergent. Centuries had passed since Sir Alexander Mackenzie had camped nearby on his search by canoe for a Northwest Passage; still, our fifty acres and the ledge and the islands, yet the home of the migrating Canada geese, never really altered.

"What do you want to do today?" Brad asked me when we got up with the dawn.

"Well, I need some more salt, pepper and allspice if we're going to dry that deer that's hanging in the cache. Someone will have to go to town."

"Let's both go—what do you say we walk? I feel like walking this morning. We'll put a pack on Bushman and take one of the Leicas. How does that strike you?"

"Wonderful," I said. "If you'll water and feed the horses, I'll start breakfast. Then we can be there and back before the work on the road begins for the day. I heard that they're going to be blasting today by that brook just beyond our property: it's even beginning to bother Cloud. But they want to get as much done as possible before winter."

"Winter," he said, "when most of this *progress* shuts down, is getting to be my favorite season."

I wondered again if eventually we'd really have to move. Neither of us wanted to leave Hudson Hope, the Peace, our sourdough friends, and all the wilderness nooks that the coming multitudes, keeping to the roads as they always do, could be expected never to intrude upon. If only there weren't too many roads! Then we were walking up the trail to town and my mind settled on the task of keeping up with Brad.

Even though he was just ambling this morning, his stride was longer than mine, sure if uneven—just as the ruts were uneven—just skimming the ground, so that he covered a lot of space with less effort. He was softly humming "Make Believe"; it was evident that he didn't mind whether he was first or second, nor very much where his long legs were taking him. Still, he, and he alone, was the reason we were in the wilderness. It was he who had the determination and the will power to change our well-hidden dreams into realities.

A small flock of gulls, wheeling like scraps of paper caught up by a gust, passed so close overhead that the round eye of the leader seemed to be peering at me. A few flew here each summer, although the Pacific Ocean, across the Alaska panhandle, was 300 miles away. They always seemed to bring the cold smell of salt water with them.

"They'll be flying back to the Inside Passage soon," Brad noted. "And see those red-winged blackbirds. They're passing through again."

The blackbirds, with their red and yellow epaulets, were clustering atop browning strands of grass beside the trail. They flung themselves, with a liquid gurgling, into the air as we passed. High above them, an alert group of crows departed from the lofty dead branches of a cottonwood with a harsh cawing, leaving a stillness that was disturbed only by the humming of yellow jackets repairing a papery gray nest which looked as if it had been swiped by the paw of a hungry bear.

A low-lying cloud immersed us once we passed the oat field at the bottom of the road-festooned bluffs just north of Dudley's cabin, but our feet continued to find the trail. A half mile further along I heard wagon wheels clattering over ruts, the nearby creak of harness, and the sharp piercing ring of a horseshoe against a stone. Then the cloud began to thin out, without perceptible movement, and I could make out the shapes of Hudson Hope's dwellings.

Where there was a current of air above the great gushing spring, the warm dilution of the rising sun suddenly made itself felt. An outpouring of color illuminated the structures and bannered with yellow the smokes that were lifting straight upward. The window glass of numerous trailers in a field became dazzles of reflected sunlight. A mud-spattered truck swerved into the wide line of similar vehicles in front of the barroom and a burst of laughter from inside made Bushman prick his gray ears.

The white-fenced Hudson's Bay Company compound was blank and empty, with unattended yellow-brown grass lifting high above its elevated wooden walks. So we turned left toward Noel Verville's store. There were two stores in town now, but we found a kindred spirit in Noel, an old sourdough who'd prospected and traded on the Mackenzie River. Advancing age and the loss of an eye had turned him toward this new boomtown.

A pack of small dogs taunted Bushman but, carrying his pack with an attitude that implied dignified responsibility, the wolfhound paid them no heed.

"What do you think of Hudson Hope now?" Brad asked me. Among a knot of boisterous people in the streets, we saw no one we knew. Then Noel's bulk appeared in his doorway. Instead of the familiar fragrance of lodgepole pine, there was the smell of Canadian gasoline, raw from the pump in front of the store where Noel started to turn the handle. His body reflected a moving shadow on his square plate glass window, full of the late sunrise.

The day had brightened so, by the time we got back to the cabin, that we decided to let the deer hang another day and, instead, to ride into the still uninvaded forest atop the hills behind the cabin. We'd saddled Cloud and Chinook and tied them by their reins to small poplars—around which grew berry bushes whose sweetness they liked to nip—while I fixed lunch.

I'd just noticed from the east window that Cloud had stepped over his reins. I was starting out to untangle him when there was an explosion. Workmen were dynamiting a road through a shale ledge, across the brook just beyond the western edge of our fifty acres. The gray gelding gave a startled leap forward. The sapling bent beneath his weight and he went to one knee. When he got up again he was standing on three legs, shivering. The reins had been wound around his left foreleg in such a way that, in combination with his weight and the bending poplar, it had broken his ankle.

I might have screamed, except that it took a moment for everything to sink in. Then there was only one thing to do. I was crying when Brad, rifle in hand, led him away; Cloud still trembling with shock, and probably not feeling any pain yet, and hopping along on three legs. I knew Brad would take him far enough into the woods where the other creatures could scour his bones. Even though we loved Cloud we felt nothing should be wasted. Horseflesh in the belly of some wolves or a bear might save the life of a moose.

Then I heard the shot. I remembered that the gentle, usually placid gray had always been a little gunshy, and that started the tears again. Then Brad came back alone, unsaddled Chinook and put her in the corral, replaced the rifle on the two long spikes that supported it above the door, and held me for long seconds without saying a word.

Then he said, "The Matsons are leaving the Hope. Too much civilization. Going up to the Liard River. Their daughter has a young, copper-colored mare that's a pet."

"I n-never want another horse."

"I was thinking of getting her, anyway," Brad went on. "We can always use her for a pack animal to bring in game. Got the lunch ready?"

I nodded against his shoulder, the tears still coming.

"We've got to be doing something, honey," he said, his cheek against mine. "Let's take the boat upriver. We've always been wanting to explore Starfish Creek and I can't think of a better time."

Later I said, "Why are you taking the gun? I don't want us to kill anything if we don't have to."

"With that grizzly in the country," he said, "it's just as well to have a rifle. We might not be so lucky a second time. Do you want to take Bushman?"

"I just want there to be you and me."

"All right, honey," he said.

With almost physical agony, I twisted my mind away from emptiness and nothingness to the beauty of the sunlit wilderness. To the living strength of the river. To the companionship of the only friend who really mattered. Several miles upriver, the clear day gleamed like fire on a break in the bluffs that marked the start of Starfish Canyon.

Up the rocky south shore about a mile and a half from the head

Northern legends say that the early autumn river mists are made up of the ghosts of oldtime voyageurs and sourdoughs.

King Gething's wilderness coal mine on Bullhead Mountain.

Brad atop Mt. Selwyn.

of Box Canyon, I remembered from trips along the opposite shore, was a creek canyon. It was a chasm almost as deep as the bed of the Peace River itself, heading into the mountains to the south. On those winter days when we'd been able to reach it on the ice, it had been too drifted over with snow to follow without snowshoes, which we never carried when traveling the river.

The slim canyon, through which a shallow stream twinkled, had always intrigued me. Near its mouth and on the northern side of the river, too, fossil starfish were to be found. My prize discovery so far was a small, multilaminated slab of sandstone: in it was a large parent echinoderm, surrounded by numerous tiny starfish, golden as the adhesive stars found on Sunday School records. The slab, I had discovered by cautious chipping, was filled with these tiny yellow fossils.

Now Brad and I ventured between huge towering bluffs of shale, gravel and rocks into a narrow gorge. On the eastern side of it was a grassy stretch, cool beneath cottonwoods, tracked by passing moose, deer, wolves, coyotes, bear, beaver and smaller forest folk. For maybe ten minutes we threaded along the deep, dim aisle between nearly perpendicular walls. Then the choked passage twisted, the sides flared, and where there had been one stream and one canyon, there were now two. More tracks had followed the gorge to the right, so that was the desolation we chose.

Stones, slags and boulders were bound together by crumbling shale into an ever-dusting, patternless, tilted, ravaged monotony of grandeur whose floor had been smoothed, in a manner of speaking, by centuries of trickling water. We were probably the first human beings to invade here since, perhaps, a solitary prospector at the turn of the century, tarrying to pan the Peace River on his way overland from Edmonton to join the Klondike Stampede.

Here, in the secret interior hollowness of Rocky Mountain Canyon's gaunt and skeletal fastness, unscalable cliffs lifted to a tableland thick with poplar. A few of the trees had been sucked inexorably over the eroding sides. A banner of dust 800 feet above us shone in the sun. In the slit of daylight high above our heads, I could see an osprey gliding with crooked wings. The only walking now was single file in the water itself, Brad leading the way. Our rubber-bottomed leather boots made scarcely a sound.

As I picked a path around the continuing curve of the narrow canyon, now busy with willow on its western side, rock fell with an echo somewhere in the shadows. A cold breeze scooped up the pulverized, dry particles of surrounding earth, as a slide clattered up ahead. The boulders in the bottom were unwieldy now and the stream, the only way among them, the merest thin milk-gray thread among the tumbled, ruined, slanting mass of confusion.

It was so unnerving that, remembering all too well how we'd once been trapped underground in the old Allard-Gething coal mine upriver, I wished I hadn't come. But the savagery of the narrow passage kept luring me onward. I hurried to get away from a sudden thickness of willow. Wind hit me in the face and the shadows were cold. Because of the way the rocks, shale and miniature torrent narrowed and twisted, I couldn't see more than a few feet ahead. I came around another turn, and there was a grazing moose.

The bull, for that was what it was, looked enormous. I could see his heavy slanting back and powerful hindquarters. He was gnawing on a sparse stand of green-leaved willows that stuck out of the western shale wall.

Then he flung up his head and looked around. Surprised, the animal turned almost in his tracks to face us. Following the example of Brad, into whom I bumped, I froze.

The bull's nose extended warily. He had probably never seen a human before. Icy wind blew down the canyon toward us and turned his breath to vapor.

Sniffing noisily, the huge animal stepped toward us. My impulse was to flee, but I knew that would be the worst move I could make.

"If you ever get in a tight spot with an unharmed wild animal," Brad had told me more than once, "usually the worst thing you can do is run. That way you're making up the beast's mind, because then its natural reaction is to chase."

The moose took another step forward. A grunt that was more like a growl rumbled past yellow teeth. The long, coarse hair on the top of his neck lifted. I tried to remind myself that healthy, unprovoked wild animals, with the occasional exception of grizzly and polar bears, won't attack you. But my hands were clammy and I had trouble keeping my knees steady.

Here in the narrow creek bottom there was no room for us to maneuver. There was no shelter. The rubbly sandstone walls offered no holds. Brad half lifted his rifle and I heard the bolt snick as he levered a cartridge into the barrel. But even if we had wanted to kill this moose, which we didn't, we were at too close quarters for shooting.

"Get back," Brad said in a low voice to me. "Easy."

Following his example, I started to sidle back the way we had come.

The moose, still trying to get our smell, was moving toward us faster now. The gorge angled in such a way that, to keep us in view, the bull would have to shorten the gap between us more and more.

I could feel my heart thumping. Our choice of action was becoming very limited. Whether the bull should decide that we were something to drive away with flashing forefeet, or just an obstruction to be dashed aside, would make little difference.

Brad decided on what seemed to be the most conservative thing he could do. He stepped slowly back toward the moose, careful not to startle him into action by any sudden move. It might work.

It didn't. The bull moose grunted with displeasure and came on.

I kept watching him closely, in case we'd have to try to jump aside at the last minute. We both must have remembered another axiom at the identical instant—we'd had to use it before: the most soothing thing a man can do when he's cornered is to begin talking quiet and easy; the sound of such a human voice sometimes has a calming effect on a wild animal. Brad started talking now. His voice seemed dry at first and I could feel him trying to keep his tones calm. The words sounded hoarse and unreal to me, but the moose stopped.

Still talking—now, I realized, just calling signals as he would have in football but in a quiet voice—he said, "Easy now, moose. No one wants to hurt you. Eighteen, twenty-four, forty-one, sixteen . . . ."

We were both backing up. I retreated behind Brad step by step, while the bull watched.

Then a clay-coated stone shifted beneath my weight. I stumbled. My other foot hit spray-slicked rocks and I fell backward.

I heard a rumbling grunt and the startled clatter of hooves. The dark, menacing antlers drove into view. Half a ton of muscle and bone was charging. Loose shale slipped beneath me as I scrambled to get on my feet.

The sound of the shot deafened me. At these close quarters, not wanting to obscure his view with the fixed telescopic sight, Brad had only half raised his .30-06. Now the bull shuddered, reeled against the opposite wall, then rebounded to fall in the middle of the creek. Muddy water began to build up behind him.

Brad had already jacked another cartridge into the chamber and was ready for a finishing shot. But none was necessary. The bull's eyes were already glazing over. That 180-grain Peters bullet, we found later, had severed the jugular and broken the neck, part of it then splitting off to range downward through the heart and liver.

"It had to be a brain or a spine shot at that distance," was all Brad said.

"Why did it ever act that way?"

"This canyon must come to a dead end a short way upstream," he said, and we subsequently proved him correct. "He was cornered."

18

Copper

Brad bought a new horse for me, a mare like the older Chinook—who quickly reestablished her leadership as she had with Cloud. Where the new mare's coat wasn't already becoming shaggy with winter hair, it gleamed like a newly coined penny, so I named her Copper. She had been a pet and she nuzzled my neck when I turned after giving her her first bundle of oats. I had a hopeful, beginning feeling about it. We decided to let her get used to us by riding together upriver. We'd head for where the trail ended at a riverside cliff at Gold Bar, twenty miles beyond the upper end of the portage.

We each rolled food and few personal items into a mummy-sized down sleeping bag. We packed them behind the cantles of our comfortable western saddles, and we took Bushman.

"Shall we padlock the cabin?" I asked Brad doubtfully.

"We'd better now," he said after a moment. "There are so many strangers around. Seems odd, doesn't it? We used to leave it unlocked year after year."

The past few days, Brad had been bringing in the moose from Starfish Creek; I'd been drying and canning both it and the venison we already had. Nothing had disturbed the entrails in the canyon except eagles, Brad said. One of them had nearly buffeted him with its wings, struggling to become airborne when he unexpectedly rounded the narrow corner. He'd never realized the eagles which rode the air currents in these mountains were so immense.

As we rode through Hudson Hope, the black early morning sky

was paling, taking on the aspect of distant smoke. For the moment, no color showed anywhere: the buildings and trailers looked like chalk sketches on a gray pad. Somehow it seemed more like night than day, although not actually like any moment of dusk or dawn. But no sunrise I'd ever experienced was lovelier than when the gray dense gloom, like a negative, developed almost imperceptibly into a honeywarm haze. Not yet sure of myself on this new mount, I kept my eyes on Copper's ears as the town came up around us.

The hush of the dawn enveloped us and in it small sounds built suddenly. A heavy man, whose folded-back sleeves and muscular forearms spoke of trucking, was thumping down the wooden sidewalk between Miller's poolroom and the bar. I thought of Dawson Creek: when Brad and I had first seen the town where the Alaska Highway now started, it had been two muddy streets with high wooden sidewalks; somehow now it seemed it was a city.

Larry Gething was driving his small herd of cattle from the barnyard down to the spring. I could hear the heavy, unhurried rhythm of their breathing and the lean suction of their hooves in a stretch of mud. Larry, a tall handsome man with graying hair, lifted a friendly hand.

"He probably won't be able to do that much longer," Brad told me. "People are already talking about a herd law for Hudson Hope. No more stock running free."

"Will that affect us?" I asked.

"It'll mean that the next time we have to go to the States for university or library research on a new book, we won't be able to put our horses out to graze."

"What can we do with them?"

"Rent pasture space somewhere," he said.

Copper was proving to be lazy, which Cloud had never been, and it was hard to make her trot side by side with Chinook. Heeling her did little good and I didn't want to begin wearing spurs. I reached out and broke off a willow switch. I found I could get the best results just by letting Copper see it out of the corner of her eye. Evidently she was an animal of vigorous imagination.

The forests had been thinning out with the approach of another winter, but already the cool, shadowed air was becoming warmer in the breezeless dawn. The tree trunks were beginning to gleam yellowly and, where we passed a stand of lodgepole pine on the slope below the pioneer cemetery, there was a warming resinous aroma. Kinnikinic berries glowed redly; above them, the tall fireweed was shriveling, having already gone to white-parachuted seeds. I felt the reaching, waiting stir inside me of coming winter.

The town fell behind as we rode higher, into the lifting dawn. The poplars were turning to gold and occasionally there was a small lone tree, its leaves a collection of freshly minted coins againt the blue sky. Even the birch leaves were rusting, but so far there was no gleam to them. The hardwoods on the slopes to the river trembled and quivered in the incessant air currents that followed the whitened green water; only the spruce and the pines stood erect, nothing but their dull verdant crowns wavering with a slow reflective sway of branches.

The whole country seemed moody with the biting lateness of autumn, as if it were inhaling the clean sharpness of the air: Copper, Bushman and Chinook moved with deliberate prudence in it. To the north, just before Portage or Four Mile Creek that had flowed beside the clearer Bull Creek by our original homesite, was a long bulldozed strip with an air sock.

"The new airfield," Brad said. "It even accommodates jets."

"I read somewhere that Alaska already has more private planes than any other state," I said. "How would it be, moving to Alaska? You know we considered that at first."

"Homesteading is stopping in Alaska, not that we'd necessarily want to homestead," Brad said. "But most of the vast government wildernesses are tied up in the courts, partly because of native claims. The Division of Lands in Anchorage does conduct periodic sales of state-owned land: that might do if there was something we wanted and we were on the spot. There are also occasional sales of borough-owned lands; anyone can usually get advance information on them from the Division of Lands. But private sales are the most common there, and they're becoming more and more expensive."

"It's such a magnificent place, what we've seen of it," I said.

"Yes," he said, "and the vast majority of the people who are closing it up will never even take the trouble to go there for a visit. Maybe that will protect the pristine qualities of the area, though. What's bothering the horses?"

I realized Copper was dancing and arching her neck. Then I

saw a glossy, dark shape ripple sleekly across the road, streak up a small pine for a sharp-faced scrutiny, then dart back down and out of sight.

"That was a fisher," Brad said excitedly. "They're members of the weasel family and the most valuable of all Hudson Hope's fur."

Near the end of the portage, the shore again dipped down to what was a mostly placid river from there on. A new, heavily traveled, gravel road branched off to the left. It followed what had been a trail bulldozed in to the canyon bank a few years ago, when Lloyd Gething, King's younger brother, was mining coal on Bullhead under a lease from Les Allard, who had a crown grant there. This was where work was now taking place on the big new earth dam. It would be one of the largest in the world and would back the wilderness river up the breadth of the Canadian Rockies and up the feeding Parsnip and Finlay Rivers. The latter were in the Continental Trough, where there was talk of running a railroad to the Yukon Territory.

"Want to ride over and see what's happening?" Brad asked.

"Not particularly."

Overhead, a scattering of high-flying sandhill cranes hyphened downriver.

"They're getting an early start," Brad said, his blue eyes narrowing as he squinted upward. "Must be storms where they started from—the Yukon probably, or maybe Alaska."

The season was more advanced the further we rode upriver. The trees were becoming barer, only the bearberry bushes below still carrying their crimson blush of leaves. A strange vision came into my mind. Once man, armed only with clubs and spears, had moved stealthily, vulnerable, among tremendous forests of towering trees. Now, in the too-profuse cities and suburbs, fewer and fewer trees stood vulnerable amid forests of indifferent people.

We had lunch by a stream: moose kabobs bitten directly from green wands while they still sizzled. Then we rode on. There were so many varying hares—who had eaten vast stretches of shrubbery bare as high as they could reach—that Bushman finally lost interest in them! As evening approached, the country opened up where it had been cleared by fire during spring after spring. We saw cattle browsing on an open hillside, the waning light washing the white on their bodies to platinum.

Copper settled down into an easy pace, following Chinook's lead in alternate walking and trotting. As the slow northern sunset neared, I kept closing my eyes against the slanting glare and basking in its warmth. My body relaxed, but my thoughts kept scurrying to and fro, reliving our pleasant past and feeling curiosity about our future, while the eternal watch gradually disappeared behind a craggy range.

"I think that's where Twelve Mile Creek goes north into Butler Range," Brad told me. "Jim Beattie has a second ranch and a cabin near its mouth; he's told me we're welcome to stay there any time."

The last lingering sunlight was filtering through a small stand of lodgepole pine, angling like the tight golden strings of some East Indian musical instrument. I could almost hear the vibration of a tune, and I wondered why loveliness is so much more than just something to look at. Why did it touch me so?

I dimly realized that Brad had dismounted and was holding a wire gate open for me. A few minutes later we came upon a small knot of buildings and a pole corral. After watering the horses and getting an oat bundle for each of them from the adjoining stable, we turned Chinook and Copper into the corral and unsaddled them.

The little cabin that stood on a knoll above Twelve Mile Creek had an old-fashioned sturdiness to it, right out of a Currier and Ives lithograph. At the same time, it was as pretty in the rising light of a full moon as if it had been molded in Staffordshire pottery. The latchstring was out and we went inside. Shavings and kindling were ready by the small stove, but Brad left them where they were, borrowing the ax that was stuck in a chopping block to prepare his own. Afterward, except for the snapping of the fire, silence enclosed us so completely that the munching of the horses drifted in amiably through the open doorway.

"This is going to be flooded by the dam?" I said.

"All this," he said. "Gold Bar, too. We'll see that tomorrow."

Thirty-four miles upriver from Hudson Hope, along a rambling river trail that—from the portage upward—was mainly the work of pioneer and wooden-legged Jim Beattie, was the cluster of gigantic log buildings at Gold Bar. This was the supply point for the few far-flung Peace River trappers such as our friends Leo Rutledge, Gus Krossa, Bob Yeomans, Stanley Wallace, Fred Chapman and Billy Kruger, as well as Billy, Jimmy and Bobby Beattie. All of it was to be flooded out by the future lake.

Jim Beattie's china-blue eyes examined Copper carefully for me when we arrived the next morning. His pioneer wife, Elizabeth, and their industrious daughters, Olive and Ruth, busied themselves in the spacious kitchen, readying the lunch to which Mrs. Beattie had hospitably invited us.

"Looks like a good young mare for you," Jim Beattie told me reassuringly. "Sturdy and not skittish. Dependable. That's what counts most when you're riding by yourself up in this wilderness."

He looked as if he would be efficient at running a ranch or anything else that came up.

"Glad you stayed at Twelve Mile. Why don't you try my cabin at the portage on the way home? The Gethings have a barn across from it with some hay stored there."

We made it there late that afternoon, the two horses picking up speed now that they were heading home again. The weather was so good that we picketed them outside that night, lariats hitched to a foreleg of each with a nontightening, nonjamming bowline.

We found an old curry comb in the barn. Brad used it on Chinook first, while I was getting supper. Then I took my turn with Copper. She stood easily, swaying her weight against its roughness, her coppery hide twitching with pleasure. Maybe that was why, when during the night varying hares gnawed through her older, salt-encrusted picket rope in three places, she didn't stray from Chinook.

19

Tracking Ursus Horribilis

After two weeks' work getting in the winter's meat following our return from Gold Bar, chinooks came, putting an end to Brad's hunting for the time being. The weather remained cold enough for the raw quarters we already had to keep well, hung where they were behind the cabin in the cool, airy cache.

What snow there was disappeared under the urgency of the warm dry westerlies and we started bathing in the river again. There was a placid pool behind the inland part of the great reef to which our cabin site sloped; we hastened down there with soap, towels and, now that strangers were apt to appear at any time, bathing suits. I have never felt more revitalized than after one of those dunkings.

Our formula was simple. We'd wade to where the water was waist deep, then immerse all of a sudden. Our bodies burned as if on fire while we stood behind the great stone buttress, there protected from the usual downriver wind, and soaped. Then we'd plunge in again, staying under as long as possible to wash off the last of the lather. Toweling would bring our blood rushing warmly to the surface.

We were both accustomed to what passed for cold showers in the cities, but it had never been anything like this. It wasn't bravado that made us continue this bathing as long as possible in the fall, even when we had to break through a skim of ice. It was because we felt so wonderful afterward; we were refreshed, revitalized, just as if we were beginning a new day.

Brad, after city years of writing from midnight till dawn—when the metropolis was stillest—had changed his work habits entirely and now customarily went to the typewriter directly after breakfast. He became so conditioned to this that his mind, finally, was at its most creative at this time. But then we found that he could become sluggish and stagnant in the middle of the afternoon, take one of those glacial dips in the Peace, then sit down to his typewriter as stimulated as after the most restful all-night sleep. To me, it was like starting a new day, too. That's why we always put off as long as possible in the season the regime of winter sponge baths by the stove.

Then one morning the chinook stopped with a change of wind, and snow began to fall. It snowed all day and night. The following morning the snow continued, great flakes chalking indolently through yellow sunlight. The storm finally ceased in the late afternoon, but the thermometer dropped rapidly. It seemed it was going to be the first real cold of the autumn. When we took the three buckets down for water toward evening, I noticed the river's level had fallen at least two feet.

"It must be really cold back in the mountains," Brad said, filling the pails.

Just as several years before, something, I didn't know what, awoke me suddenly that night. I listened, but everything seemed the same. Bushman was still breathing heavily with sleep, so it hadn't been him. Then I realized Brad was sitting up, also. Wordlessly, we slipped our feet into our boots and went to the large front window, the dog joining us.

A silvering of moonlight, lustrous and evanescent where it gleamed from the fresh snow, lay across the floor, keeping us from bumping into anything. Nothing seemed different through the glass and we went out on the porch, the squeaking door the only sound.

"Did something wake you up, too?" Brad asked me.

There was a not quite worried, but apprehensive, brittleness to his voice.

"Yes," I said, "but I don't know what it was."

Then in the moonlight and in a ribbon of radiance from the Northern Lights I could see that the river, where it surged over the farther edge of the ledge, seemed to have flattened. There was a strange, sparkling hush to it.

"Slush," Brad said at that moment. "Heavy slush from upriver. The river is really starting to freeze."

Now I could hear the steady silver swish.

The next morning a scintillating shimmer of mist stretched like scrim over land and river. The breakfast smoke, spraying formlessly rather than coiling from the stovepipe, expanded and mingled with it—mushroomlike. The air was motionless and when I took a deep breath the sudden bite of it made me cough.

The river seemed smothered; Chinook and Copper joined their whinnying above its slowing rush when we went to take them to the glen for water. They were standing together by the gate, near the blanket-fronted slab shelter we had built for them earlier but which they never used, although we tried to get them into that habit by feeding them there. Their heads were already turned in our direction, eyes glowing warmly in the light reflected from the snow.

"They'll be eating snow pretty soon again," Brad said. "The river won't take long now to freeze."

Both horses neck-reined, so to ride them bareback all we had to do was loosen their halter ropes. Forking his fingers in Chinook's mane, Brad swung himself onto her red back, shaggy now with winter hair. Copper, nickering, stood patiently while I accomplished the same thing on the second try. By rights, having been a dancer, I should have been more agile at it than my husband. Maybe, I thought, it was because he had more reach or more confidence.

"Smells like more snow," Brad said. "Well, that'll make it easier to snake in logs for firewood."

"I wonder what Copper will think about having a weight tied to her tail?" I said, easing myself forward on her shoulder, where the riding was smoother.

"It's a natural thing," Brad said. "She won't mind, especially if you're on her back the first few times. I'm thinking of trimming and skidding in some of the straighter spruce that the bulldozers knocked over when they were making that road behind us."

Cold descended steadily that week, surely and certainly, and the river continued its ritual of congealing. The first ice, in the still shallows along the shores, was especially interesting and perfect, being hard, dark and transparent. This, as Thoreau had found before, affords the best opportunity ever offered for examining the near bottom.

I discovered I could lie at full length on ice only an inch thick, like a skating insect on the surface of the water, and study the bottom at my leisure, like a picture behind glass. Doing this a morning or two after it had first frozen, I found that the greater part of the bubbles, which at first appeared to be within the ice, were against its under surface and that more were continually rising from the bottom.

These bubbles were from an eightieth to an eighth of an inch in diameter, very clear and beautiful, and I could see my face reflected in them through the ice. There seemed to be as many as thirty or forty of them to a square inch. Also, already within the ice, there were narrow, oblong, perpendicular bubbles, one directly above another like a string of beads. But those caught in the frozen covering were not so numerous nor obvious as those beneath. Finally, the thickening ice lost its black transparency and its beauty was gone. Brad began to carry an ax with him again when we went down to the river for water.

More snow than usual fell during that winter and it deepened with an unusual dearth of chinooks; although we crossed the tracks of a grizzly several times during the cold weather, Brad did not attempt to track it back into the bush. I thought of it more than once, though, especially during several January weeks when the slant of the sun became such that the first yellow light of the morning found the Currier and Ives lithograph on our wall, the one that Brad liked especially, a trapper fighting a towering humped bear with a knife. The pelt of such a bear would entirely cover our floor, I realized, and we could move our two black bearskins into the second room.

Then balmy day began succeeding balmy day and the great migrations of swans and geese and sandhill cranes winged north. Two Canada geese stood and sat for hour after hour on the ice, across an open rent of rapids between the central islands and the ledge, long before it was time for the river to break up. It got so that they didn't flap away, only came to their feet when, talking to them, we went down for water. Soon they would be nesting on the lower of the two rocky islands.

Because he never wore a hat, Brad had let his hair get longer than usual during the winter. Now it was time to cut it again. The morning was even warmer than usual and I established him on the sunny porch in a straight-backed chair, with a big bath towel around his neck. On his neck I was using the best available new clippers from one of the big mail-order catalogs; they didn't pull as agonizingly as the old ones had.

I was trying to make the job look professional—a publisher

wanted a photograph of Brad for the jacket of a new book—and it wasn't easy. His hair had a natural wave to it that made it stand up in back if I didn't get it just right. To see better, I leaned so close that my breathing ruffled the brown strands.

"Watch that ear," he said jokingly.

I was nervous and I guess my breath must have caught, for he looked around with a grin.

"Hold still, now," I told him, and gave the ear in question a kiss.

"Back in the city I never realized that cutting hair is so intimate," he said. "Want me to try those ends of yours? I'd be careful."

"That's woman's work," I told him. "I imagine I'd better keep on with my scissors. You can help by holding the back mirror if you will."

"Sure, Vena," he said.

"This job is coming out real nice, better than I'd expected."

"It doesn't really make much difference up here," he said. "Besides, Dudley says that there are only a couple of weeks between a poor haircut and a good one."

"Does someone do his for him?" I said.

"No, he uses a razor and a comb," Brad told me.

"Well, I'm done if it suits you." I held the large mirror in front for him, as he examined the back with the small hand mirror. "That's as good, anyway, as Mel Kyllo is doing in Miller's pool parlor."

"Thanks, dear."

A nick over his left ear made me laugh, and he caught me and kissed it from my lips. I took off the towel and shook it clean, carried the chair back inside and swept the accumulation on the planks into a dustpan, finally tilting the cuttings into the stove where they sizzled for an instant. Then I looked at my own hair, which was now shoulder length the way Brad liked it. I decided to leave it alone for at least a while longer.

A swirl of snowbirds, brown patches starting to replace their whiteness, swept away from the little food tree I kept filled with suet, cups of crumbs and, at the moment, a scattering of bright three-dimensional cookies left over from Christmas. A robin liquidly augured rain in a series of three notes, like actual drops falling.

A surf of sound awoke me at night, rain smacking on the heavy-duty asphalt roofing that Brad had used to cover Dudley Shaw's leaky shakes. For a drowsy moment I could almost smell the roasting chestnuts that enlivened the rain-spattered streets of Paris in the wintertime. But here in the wilderness the winter, with its scrubbing gales and awesome cold, was gone in the thousands of fingering raindrops. The odor I really sensed was that of the washed earth reawakening beneath its snow.

It was still raining, although more softly, in the morning. While Brad brought in firewood, I went to feed the horses, who stood with their tails to the storm and whickered their greeting. There was the muffled music of water tinkling from the ax-hollowed poplar gutters into the rain barrels: coal-oil drums with their tops neatly chiseled away. Despite the escape pole that I kept slanted in each, there was a drowned mouse in the one at the southeast corner. I eased it out with a stick, deciding that it hadn't been there long enough to foul the soft water that I used for washing.

The clay paths around the cabin were slippery and we both stepped carefully, hardly noticing the rain in our faces. Below in the open stretch of river, where rapids by the ledge had eroded the ice, big drops appeared to be bounding off the water like handfuls of new dimes. The two geese weren't there.

"The wind's from the west again," Brad said when we were back inside the cabin. I followed his gaze across river, through the streaming panes, to where the spruce and lodgepole pine were green blurs. "It's going to clear."

Rain still streaked down during eggs, Canada bacon, sourdough pancakes and coffee. The drops twisted down the glass of the picture window, making runnels that reminded me that spring housecleaning lay before me. In less than an hour, though, the clouds opened and clear golden sunlight sent no less than five separate rainbows arching among the mountains.

"Want to take a ride, Vena?" Brad asked me. "That grizzly has been up above Box Canyon and the snow will be soft for tracking. We can chain Bushman."

"Should I take my .250-3000?" I asked doubtfully.

"Too light," he said. "If there's any shooting, it's got to be heavy caliber. I'll have my .30-06, and you'd better stick pretty close. With civilization moving in, there won't be anything but the occasional grizzly around here soon. On second thought, maybe I'd better go alone today. Grizzlies are the most dangerous animals around here."

"No," I said determinedly, unable to keep the quiver out of my chin. "I'll be quiet. You're all I have."

"Sure," he said, his arm going around me. "Sure. Everything will be fine."

When he stood against the light that way, I could see Brad had become heavier during a winter of moose meat, sourdough bread, dried fruit, and the jams and jellies and wild vegetables I'd put up. But it had gone into his shoulders; his hips were leaner than ever.

"I'll saddle," he said, "while you put up the lunch. And don't forget some of that fantastic plum pudding from Boston a fan sent us for Christmas, to go with our tea."

Abetted by the swelling rain, streams were breaking loose and wearing open their courses to the Peace. They made sparkling ribbons atop the old ice and snow; when they came to the river, they expanded into gleaming pools. The springs in the cliffs beside the river, great knots of ice, were sparkling and dripping with fresh water that caught the light, even on the shadowy south side of the river. The great frozen waterfalls of Bull and Four Mile Creeks were showing rifts in their white masses and silt was spreading muddily at their bases.

Even Copper and Chinook felt the lift of spring. Just as during the start of a chinook, they threw up their heads, then curved them downward to snatch at an exposed fireweed or grab mouthfuls of water-saturated snow with exuberant snaps of yellowed teeth. They'd had an easy winter, although now they seemed to be losing weight as their shaggy coats started to shed. They pranced like colts.

A growing gale reminded me that winter still gripped the higher mountains upriver. Many of the heights were topped with permanent snowcaps and glaciers and the wind had a bite in it that I hadn't expected. I was wearing Brad's extra woolen stag shirt and I wrapped it tighter around me.

"I like that," he said appraisingly. "It makes you look more like a ballerina. The turned-up collar is a frame for your face."

"I don't know if my face will stand a frame," I said, but he just grinned.

We rode through a buttering of sunlight. I drew in a heavy breath and felt it deep within me, an inexplicable, inebriating excitement that coursed down to my feet. They set themselves more demandingly in the iron stirrups. It was wonderful to be out together again in weather somewhat similar to a chinook, but more durable, with all the haste along the clouded western horizon.

A dark shape angling up a kinnikinic-green slope of Bullhead brought me back from my reverie. But it was only a black bear, so common here that this year again there was no closed season on them. Later, a high-shouldered moose stared at us a long while before trotting away. On a river bar upstream there was movement: I thought at first it was wolves, but it turned out to be a pack of coyotes.

Up in the spruce-filled greenness of the swamp for which I have such an affection, because it's here in winter that you see the yarded moose—they tramp down a small area where they can move around and feed, in the deep forest where the chinooks don't reach to melt the snow—we found the big-toed tracks of a bear with the grizzly's long, extended nails. The marks were as fresh and sharp as those of our two horses. The tracks headed at first for the verdant inclines at the head of the basin. We'd found bear there often. They swung south to the frozen Rocky Mountain Canyon, then up the deeper snow of the opposite bank.

"Here's where we tie the horses," Brad said.

Water talked beneath the river ice as, long poles in our hands, we cautiously followed the crossing already proved by the much heavier grizzly. The rumble of a growl quickened my already hurried breathing when we were halfway up the snow-slippery shale of the south shore. It reverberated from the muskeg ahead: a spruce-clogged maze of preglacial chasms into which the sogginess of a half-dozen streams soaked.

Odd behavior? Yes, but weren't bear notoriously short-tempered when awakening for good, sluggish and parched, in the spring? Then I was scrambling behind Brad to the top. A dark bulk was disappearing into the shadowed density ahead, too late for a shot. I stared at a heavily trodden hummock that, screened by alders, had overlooked our approach.

The casualness of the afternoon was gone. That part of our most primitive ancestor which survives within each of us was coming awake with the stirring of danger. I could see that the safety of the Winchester had become reassuring beneath Brad's thumb. Even the inert trigger guard was now a cold, sure pressure against which his forefinger oriented itself.

Grizzly! Well, the 220 open-pointed grains of bullet, projected with 2830 foot pounds of muzzle energy, was enough to stop ursus horribilis or any other descendant of the bears that once prowled here with sabre-toothed tigers themselves. The claw-indented tracks stretched to over a foot in length. And here were several dark hairs, tipped with silvery grey, caught in the laxative bark (which is why bears eat it first thing in the spring) of a freshly clawed pine.

We kept softly to the more open parts of the muskeg, moving from hummock to frozen hummock. The bear never got very far ahead. I could hear the occasional rasp of its heavy paws breaking through the crusted overflow. Traveling one side or the other of the spoor began to lay pressures along my muscles, which occasionally crossing the fresh trail to check it did nothing to ease. (The good tracker doesn't directly follow a track, as the animal keeps looking back. He keeps to one side of it, occasionally rechecking its direction.) Snow and shadows were deepening. Ahead, a series of shallow beaver ponds gleamed: but before reaching them, the bear swung back into even deeper concealment. The tracks showed that it had quickened its pace to a lope.

"Well, there's always tomorrow," Brad said.

I felt more alive than I had for months as we recrossed the Peace and rode homeward.

The next morning we left both horses and Bushman at the cabin and crossed the river just below our old home site, where rumor had it that the bridge was going across. Then we climbed the creek that cut through the center of that country. The stream had frozen in a series of levels, behind fallen trees and other obstructions, so it was like silently ascending a giant staircase.

Fresh game trails were everywhere. An ermine, still white against a wet black trunk, regarded us inquisitively before gliding out of sight with a flick of jet-tipped tail. I wondered again how it was that the red squirrels could chase these deadly little creatures away from their food tree. A large silver fox drifted across a flat, his brush whisking the snow to distinguish his neat tracks from those of a small coyote.

All of a sudden we came upon two timber wolves that were following fresh moose prints up out of a coulee. They looked like gigantic, 180-pound sled dogs until you looked into their slanted yellow eyes. By that time, they were swerving back the way they'd come, running at full tilt but never in a straight line, like the shiftiest of All-American halfbacks.

The huge grizzly tracks, when we cut them among the pearl-gray poplars at a swamp's edge, set my heart pounding. Maybe there's some other brand of hunting that packs as much breath-holding excitement as stalking grizzly in soft snow, but if there is, neither Brad nor I have discovered it yet. The tracks wandered some, then headed generally west into the perfume-ladened breezes. Brad pointed to my feet, then to his ears, cautioning me to be extra quiet, but I was already being as cautious as a bush horse in a muskeg.

For an instant, as we climbed the rim of a prehistoric chasm, I had a passing vision of a chaste white mound soaring into the azure sky through the gnarled black confusion of a fallen-in forest that had been burned years ago, perhaps by Moberly Lake Indians to bring in game. The next moment Bullhead vanished, like a Disneyland king who chose to stay concealed among his courtiers until a more auspicious time. A queer sort of feeling settled in my stomach.

The grizzly had still been ambling along, chomping on the occasional rise of fresh grass. He'd tarried to investigate an old mule deer bed, now loosening its ice-embedded patches of hollow dark hair. Snow plopped as it fell from trees. I could hear sheets of ice tearing loose in the rising river. Once a massive shadow made me duck. A soaring eagle screeched.

The tracks began to lose their directness in the deepening thickness of an ancient canyon, mossier than most. Increasingly frequent crisscrossings of older footprints struck an additional warning. To our right a low ridge, remnant of an earlier stream bank, extended its eroded skeleton into the morass. Always working into the wind and careful of crumbling sandstone, we inched forward.

I heard the bear before I saw it. Alders swayed at the edge of a small opening about 150 yards away. I could see Brad centering the crosshairs of his scope on the silver-tipped shoulder about one third of the way down. I could see his forefinger start to whiten against the trigger. When the huge animal lumbered behind a stunted spruce, I could feel as well as see the tension in Brad's face as he forced himself to wait.

A low, quavering howl abruptly swelled against the stillness. It was joined by shriller, more tremulous wails. Two small shapes wrestled into view. A third romped after them.

Bony and almost hairless, the trio looked more like monkeys than the calendar pictures you see of cuddly, plump cubs. Their mother didn't seem to notice any shortcomings, though, as she touched noses with each. The three cubs were swarming all over her when we started easing back the way we had come.

20

Hollywood?

We still felt like a million dollars when, a safe distance away, we stood on a ridge and glassed the country below. It wasn't until then that I started quivering, as an aspen leaf shivers in a flutter of breeze. Brad, putting the binoculars back inside his shirt, drew me warmly down beside him on a sunlit patch of wind-dried sphagnum moss. With a great surge of mutual understanding, I took his long hard hands in both of mine.

"They won't be staying here long," he said, "once the activities reach this side of the river. As long as they can, grizzlies keep well away from people."

"I'm glad you didn't have to shoot."

"Yes," he said. "It was a touchy few minutes, even touchier than it was with that moose up Starfish Creek. Vena."

"What?"

"Nothing. I just wanted to hear myself saying your name."

I felt myself smiling.

"Vena," he said, "it's crazy, but I'm glad you saw them with me."

"I'm glad, too," I said. "It's strange, but when it was happening, I wasn't afraid." Then I asked, "Were you afraid?"

He didn't answer for a moment; then he smiled, as if at himself.

"No, not at the time," he said. "Only for the bear."

He ducked out from under the black leather strap of the binoculars so that we could take turns in looking through them.

Almost straight ahead, across the ice of the Peace River, was our cabin. I could see Bushman coiled by the dwindling woodpile and what was to be my garden plot in front and, to the right side, the brown poles of the corral with Copper and Chinook hidden by the trees between it and the river. Above all this, to the north, was the snow-patched incline of the foothills on which two moose now browsed, not far from the secret lake. No one knew about it but us because the stream that raged out of it soon disappeared underground in the willow-tangled flat below, reappearing finally as seepage in the limestone cliffs just west of our path to the ledge.

Two-and-one-half miles downriver, to the right, what had been the sparse huddle of log cabins that comprised Hudson Hope was beginning to expand into blocks and streets. More and more trailers were arriving, having a hard time of it in the spring mud after they left the Alaska Highway. There was talk of building a straighter, more gradual access from Fort St. John and hardtopping it. Men were already getting ready to survey for the new road to Chetwynd and for the proposed bridge.

"It used to take Harry Garbitt two days to reach Moberly Lake with horses," Brad said, "and from the way they're talking, trucks will soon be able to make it in about an hour."

"You don't sound very happy about it."

"Are you?" he asked. "It used to be that except for the odd Indian trapper, this south side of the Peace pretty much belonged to us. Well, I suppose we may as well be heading back to the cabin."

"At least," I said, "no one will ever be able to take this day away from us."

"No," he said. "We've had the best of it all."

Holding hands, we swung abreast down the parklike slope toward the beaver meadow. The sun was shining warm and yellow on our bare heads, twinkling in a thousand tiny sparkles in the patches of soft snow.

Water was silvering over the beaver dam, although we could still walk around the great brown mounds of beaver houses with the pussy willows growing from them and with their now-floating perimeters of moose tracks that had hardened in the refrozen snow of the pond. The beavers, who had to keep working lest their teeth grow overlong, had felled another poplar and had been cutting off the branches whose bitter, edible inner bark showed whitely.

Below the valley-wide mass of sticks and mud, a steadily eroding channel in the ice showed black with running water that
coursed among the skeletons of last year's cattails, one of the most
versatile of the edible wild plants.

"It's about time we went on another food-hunting expedition," I
said.

"As soon as the snow goes," he promised. "We'd better ride
into town this afternoon for the mail."

"That's right," I said. "I forgot it's mail day."

"Don't make a slip," he cautioned. "Not a word about the grizzlies."

"I wouldn't for the world," I said.

"I know you wouldn't on purpose," he said, giving my hand a
squeeze. "But weren't they really something!"

There was a mass of mail, as usual: among the letters for Brad,
one with a red and black heading stood out—from Associated
Publications at Rockefeller Center in New York City. The firm
published a string of motion picture trade magazines with sec-
tional inserts. When we'd lived in Boston, Brad had been New
England Editor for several years. Ben Shylen, the publisher and
owner, was offering him the job of heading up the all-important
Hollywood office.

"I've never met Mr. Shylen," I said when we were talking
about it on the ride back to the cabin.

"He's the cleverest man in the business," Brad said, "and you
can see that he expects to pay."

"It stands to reason he must be clever." I felt my face getting
warm. "But, in a way, wouldn't it be like swapping the shadow of
possibility for the substance of probability?"

"It's a pretty solid possibility," he said.

"But could Mr. Shylen be expected to stand by you if things go
wrong? That's something the wilderness will always do."

I was still thinking of it that night in my sleeping bag. Drowsi-
ness just wouldn't come. I kept seeing my slim, erect dancer's
body in the mirror where I'd been tying back my hair; the swirling painted skirt and the green lace blouse from a trip to Mexico
City; the tanned, somehow heart-shaped face; the overlarge
mouth, the too small nose and the too widely spaced hazel eyes,
then still and somehow eloquent. Hollywood would give me a
chance, too, to go back to my profession.

Then I thought of how dependent we were upon each other
here, of how often in show business the demands of differing

careers set up marital discords. I was very afraid that if we took our love out of the Far North, it might, slowly and irretrievably, fade away like an echo.

I tried to lose the fantasy in the subdued thunder of the river and in Bushman's heavy breathing. Then I realized that the usual deep breathing of Brad was absent. When I turned my head enough to look at him next to me, there was enough moonlight for me to see that his eyes were open, too, and on me. He reached over then.

"Darling," he said. "You can't sleep, either?"

21

Fireweed

Brad was seated on the pole settee he had built on the porch. With his feet on the rail, I wondered what he was framing so intently with the toes of his moccasins. Then I saw the moose and her tiny calf. The cow, high in the water, was swimming backward down through the swollen rapids past the ledge, in such a way that the small tan body beside her was pressed protectively against her brownish-black side. It was as exciting as watching a ballerina execute an exhausting series of *fouettes* in Tschaikovsky's *Swan Lake*.

"Where do you suppose they'll land?" I asked from inside the screen door.

"Probably they'll get in that backwater behind the islands," Brad said, "and come ashore about where we do at the beaver creek; the first place they talked about putting across a bridge. It would seem strange to have a bridge in there."

"Now they seem to be talking mostly about those ledges a few hundred yards down from our first cabin," I said, and added:

"where the water is so turbulent through that little gap that you'd think the ice would never back up there and freeze first, but it always does, like a cork in a bottle."

"It'll seem strange anywhere," Brad said, and he swung his feet to the floor. "I can understand how Daniel Boone, Davy Crockett and some of those old pioneers used to feel when civilization followed them west," he said, a faraway look in his blue eyes. "Yes, we'll have to move north if we go."

I went out and stood beside him, but we couldn't see the two moose any more. I felt the flanneled hardness of one of his arms go around my shoulders.

"I don't want to go to Hollywood," I heard myself saying.

"I know," he said very softly. "After last night I know."

"Brad," I said. "Brad, dear. What's happened to us?"

"A very fundamental thing, Vena," he said. "We've reverted to our ancestors. The wilderness has caught us, too, in its very real spell. I can't leave it, either."

Then I realized that my cheeks were wet with tears.

"We won't have to leave it," I vowed. "If we have to go from here, we'll find some other place."

The pinkness of the dawn-suffused river was shining like the inside of a freshly sautéed Dolly Varden trout. As I watched it, almost unseeing, a movement caught the corner of my eye, appearing so suddenly that Bushman stood, staring, until Brad could grasp his collar.

A plump brown muskrat, followed by a long, thin black tail, appeared abruptly on the path.

"This must be our day!" Brad said. "Hold Bush while I get my camera."

At the squeak of the screen door the musquash, in no hurry, turned and waddled back down toward the ledge. He moved slowly enough for Brad to get several closeups of him before he slipped into the stillness of our river batheing pool, so sleekly that the action scarcely made a ripple. Only then did Bushman begin to bark.

"This must be our day," Brad said again, returning. "What say we ride up past Box Canyon and look for wild vegetables? I couldn't possibly sit south of the typewriter this morning and concentrate."

"Will there be any danger of meeting that grizzly up there?" I wondered.

"Not much," he said. "She's not apt to swim the river when it's at this stage and leave the three cubs behind. Besides, there are too many people on this side."

The first spring green we stopped to gather was some of the burdock that had sprung up near our original home site at the mouth of Bull Creek, back where we had thrown up a pole corral for the horses. This member of the thistle family marched across Europe with the Roman legions, sailed to the New World with the early settlers, and now thrives throughout much of the United States and southern Canada wherever people and their animals live. A topnotch wild food, it has the advantages of being familiar and of not being easily mistaken for anything else. When the aspiring medicine men of some of the Indian tribes tasted the weed, they sometimes drank the bitter brew of burdock, which was supposed to help them learn better and retain the acquired lore.

The somewhat unpleasant associations (burrs all over your clothing) with its name are, at the same time, often a disadvantage when it comes to bringing this aggressive but delicious immigrant to the table. Muskrats are sold in some markets as swamp rabbits, while crows find buyers as rooks. But, unfortunately, on this continent burdock is usually just burdock, despite the fact that we've seen varieties of it cultivated as prized domestic vegetables in Japan and elsewhere in the Orient.

No one need stay hungry very long where the burdock grows, for this versatile edible will furnish a number of different delicacies. Although we didn't bother with them today, it is for the roots, for instance, that they are grown by the Japanese. Only the first-year roots should be used, but these are easy to distinguish, as the biennials stemming from them have no flower and burr stalks. Other times I've exposed the tender pith of these roots by peeling, then sliced it like parsnips and simmered it for twenty minutes in water with about one-quarter teaspoon of baking soda added. Then drain, barely cover with fresh boiling water, add a teaspoon of salt and cook until tender; serve with butter or margarine.

If they are caught early enough—and this year we had done just that—the velvety smooth, although slightly woolly, young leaves can be boiled twice, using different water each time, and served as greens. If you're hungry, the peeled young leaf stalks are good raw, especially with a little salt. They can also be added to vegetable soups or cooked by themselves like asparagus.

"Let's save these for salad," I enthused.

"Fine by me," he agreed.

It is the rapidly growing flower stalk that furnishes one of the tastier parts of the burdock. When these sprout up the second year, watch them so that you can cut them off just as the blossom heads are starting to appear, as these were now. Every shred of the strong, bitter skin would have to be peeled off, I knew, but that would be easy back in my kitchen. Then I'd cook the remaining thick, succulent interiors, changing the water as I would for the roots, and serve them hot with margarine.

"Look at that bank beaver down there on our old ledge."

A large, plump animal weighing perhaps thirty pounds, with a broad black tail, was ambling unconcernedly across the fossil-embedded rock. As we watched, it reentered the water gradually because of the slant of the projection, and was soon swimming with its webbed feet up toward Box Canyon, its glossy head cleaving a white V in the river.

"Didn't I say that this is our day?" Brad asked. "Let's leave the cayuses here in our old corral and walk up to the source of Bull Creek. It's only a couple of miles and I've got Bush's pack in one of my saddlebags."

"The lunch and tea pail are in mine," I added.

We gathered some young fireweed on the way, finding the tender young stalks and leaves growing where great stands of the plant had given an unforgettable amethyst hue to the country the summer before. Fireweed is another wild vegetable difficult to mistake for anything else. Thousands of square miles of burned lands, from the Aleutians and Greenland to Mexico, soften to magenta annually, so showily do these tall perennials flame into spikelike clusters of flowers.

"I'll pan-steam these leaves tonight with margarine," I told Brad. "About four loose cupfuls will do for us, so that you'll know when you come to write about it. I'll melt two tablespoons of margarine in our biggest frypan over high heat, then stir in the greens and three tablespoons of water. Then all I'll have to do is cover them and give them a stir now and then until they're wilted, salting and peppering them to taste at the end. We'll eat them while they're still hot and savory."

"Try cutting some of the young stems into sections, too, and simmering them in a small amount of salted water until they're tender," he suggested. "I had some this way up on the Grand Cascapedia River while salmon fishing on the Gaspé Peninsula, one spring. There the French Canadians call them *asperge*—wild asparagus."

The balmy green light that sifted between the young poplar leaves as we ascended the brook began losing its verdancy, then became chilly. Although there was no sign of wind in the forest, what had been a necklace of clouds looped across the horizon began to cover the entire sky overhead. A single shadow, like a thing alive, sped up the eastern flank of Bullhead before the closely following sunlight replaced it. Then darkening clouds began somersaulting their shadows over the entire woods.

Still, a breezeless stillness expanded over the wilderness; more and more like the heavy, airless, breath-denying, yawning emptiness that comes in the moments before a hurricane explodes in all its fury. The only sound, beside that of the little stream, was a robin tut-tut-tutting in a nearby tree. The starkness all about was like a woodcut in an old book of fairy stories.

From the distance, high on the mountain, came the mutter of wind and, nearer, the first whisper of breezes. Then, all of a sudden, the woods trembled with the foreboding low rumbling that accompanies hard rain, but there was no rain—just a rising wind. Black clouds were heaping low over the woods and the thunder in their midst was becoming more ominous. We were in a fallen old burn. Grasping my hand, Brad started to run.

"Let's get out of this," he said.

Suddenly we came to a clearing where grass had taken over from the forest. Along its rim the spruce were swaying violently, then they straightened back into the sky and the evergreens to the east bent over. Lightning zigzagged nearby, thunder erasing its agitation immediately, and in the sound I heard and saw trees uprooting and crashing. A few feet away, a small limber birch whipped in the tumult. It took all our strength and balance to reach it.

"Hold onto this," Brad yelled into my ear. He stood behind me, making a cage of his body and arms. The swirling wind, driving my clothes against me, forcing my breath back into my lungs and almost pressing me off my feet, made the tiny supple birch writhe like a thing alive. Bushman silently pressed between us.

I had the fleeting hope that the horses were all right, but we had left them among small birch, too. Then the turbulence was gone as swiftly as it had come, although I could still hear it writhing and rumbling downriver.

"Whew," Brad said, releasing his hold on the tree but still standing with his warm strength sheltering me. "Wasn't that something? The wilderness never does anything halfway."

"Shall we still go on looking for food?" I asked, feeling for a comb.

"Might as well," he said. "The wind's all over with, but the afternoon is only half gone. We're almost at the start of the creek, and there are cattails there."

"It gave a kind of leafy freshness to the air, didn't it?" I said. "Just as if everything had been cleaned with electricity."

Bull Creek welled up in a basin green with tall grass, bordered with yellow arnica daisies and blossoming wild strawberries. A stand of cattails moved continuously in the draft that came down the bare sides of the cell from a western slope. I knew from our past travels that the slope led to the open ridge kniving to Larry Gething's abandoned trapping cabin on his brother King's mine road.

The spring that gushed out of the ground glittered like diamonds over moss and cress. When I eased myself down beside Brad, the turf was resilient beneath me and the water I cupped up with my joined palms was glacial.

After lunch, with the campfire warming my hands, we gathered the versatile cattails. Who does not know these tall strap-leaved plants with their brown sausagelike heads? Growing in large groups from two to nine feet high, they are exclamation points in wet places throughout the temperate and tropical countries of the world. Of course, what we looked for now were the new young plants, growing among the snow-bent and broken remnants of last year's crop.

Although now relatively unused in the United States and Canada, cattails are deliciously edible both raw and cooked, from their starchy roots to their cornlike spikes. Furthermore, the long slender basal leaves, dried and then soaked to make them pliable, provide rush matting for chairs, as well as tough material for mats. As for the fluff of the light-colored seeds, which enliven many a winter wind, these will softly fill pillows and provide warm stuffing for comforters. Incidentally, this once-important Indian food, now too often neglected except by nesting birds, is also known in some localities as rushes, cossack asparagus, bulrushes, cat-o'-nine-tails, reed mace or flags.

We sought only three parts this day. First, the tender young shoots, somewhat resembling cucumbers in taste, which I planned to use that evening in a salad. When peeled of their outer rind, it is the tender white insides of the now foot-long young stems that, both raw and cooked, give this worldwide delicacy its provocative name of cossack asparagus. Finally, there were the pithy little tidbits, where the new green stems sprout out of the rootstocks, which can be roasted or boiled like young potatoes. We soon had all of everything we could use.

Later in the year we'd gather the greenish-yellow flower spikes, before they became tawny with pollen, and drop them into rapidly boiling salted water to simmer until tender. Or perhaps, I thought now, I'd steam them to retain even more of their goodness. We'd then eat them like corn, dripping with some of Claire Barkley's butter or with store margarine. Or I'd scrape these cooked flower buds from the wiry cobs and use them like hot corn kernels.

These flower spikes later are gilded with thick pollen which, easily and quickly rubbed or shaken into a container, is a flour substitute for breadstuffs. It can be cleaned if necessary by passing it through a sieve. For delectable golden hot cakes, just mix it half and half with the regular flour in any pancake recipe.

Chinook and Copper, ears pricked, nickered at our approach. We quickly saddled them, transferred the wild edibles from Bushman's pack to the four saddlebags, and were trotting homeward, making occasional detours to avoid tangles of trees across the trail. The sinking sun burned on our necks. Somewhere back on Bullhead, a wolf howled.

22

Up the Peace River

"Progress," the newcomers—but not many of the sourdoughs—were saying.

"Yes, if inventing gunpowder was progress," Brad said.

Men, trailers, machinery, roads and all the rest were everywhere. To a lot of the tourists especially, it was all as fascinating as the innards of a piano are to a small boy who is seeing one tuned for the first time.

There were the white winters after that day of the wind storm, then the green springs, the nigh day-long radiance of summer after summer, then the golden light of another autumn. The thick earthen dam, one of the hugest in the world, was nearly ready. The Peace River, from the head of Rocky Mountain Canyon upward through the entire breadth of the Canadian Rockies and deep up and down the Continental Trough, was about to be flooded.

"Pilgrims are thinking that it's going to be another pleasure lake," King Gething, whose experience as a boatman had brought him the cognomen of King of the River, told us. "But it's going to be clogged with uprooted trees, half-sunken deadheads, logs and debris for years. And they're forgetting the winds that will burst down through the mountains. With such a mess of floating wreckage blocking the shores, there will be no shelter."

"That bad?" Brad said.

King's long, intelligent face was somber as he nodded. His deep brown eyes seemed a little darker than they had been before. He was tall and lank, stooped like a scholar, and a day's stubble of thin black beard somehow strengthened the long boniness of his jaw.

"Worse if anything," King said. "Have you two climbed Mount Selwyn yet? It's right below where the Finlay and the Parsnip Rivers meet in the Continental Trough to form the Peace."

"Just Bullhead," I said.

"Is that where Finlay Forks is?" Brad asked.

"Actually," King said, "the Forks are up the Finlay a bit. All that riverbottom is going to be flooded. I'm going to make one last trip up that way before freezeup to see old friends and stake some more claims. How would you two like to come along? We could camp across at Wicked River long enough for you to climb Selwyn if you want."

Brad and I exchanged looks.

"When," he was asking the next instant, "do we leave?"

"Well," King said, "my outfit's across the portage, all except the grub. I should get over there a few days early and do some work on the engine and a bit of caulking. How's about a week today? Dad had to go over that way to get some things out of our old cabin, where Twelve-Mile Davis used to have his trading post. He'll probably be glad to have you ride along."

"What'll we do with Copper and Chinook?" I asked.

"My brother Larry is looking after the cattle anyway," King said, "and two horses wouldn't be much extra bother. Why not speak to him?"

"How long were you figuring on being gone?" Brad said.

"Ten days should give us time for everything," King contemplated and then he smiled. "No use in hurrying."

"We'll take care of the grub," I said. "Is there anything in particular you like?"

"So long as there's plenty of tea," King said, "I can keep happy. Better take along a .22 to get rabbits for Bushman."

"Oh," I said, dropping a hand to the wolfhound's neck, "can we bring Bush?"

"He'll enjoy it, too," King said, "and he can help you pack up Selwyn."

"Is that a one or two-day trip?" Brad wanted to know.

"Selwyn rises right out of the river," King said, "and you could make it easy in a day. But it'd be an experience, camping up there overnight. Better bring a small tent if you have it. The weather that high is chancy and it's the highest mountain around. Mummy bags would be good, too."

"We're all set then, if it's all right with your Dad and Larry," Brad told him. "Unless something gets in the way, we'll see you one week from today, King."

The weather continued stimulatingly chill and golden. In the gleam of lamplight from our picture window, we saw a spider attaching an anchor thread to a withered fireweed the night before we were to leave.

"More good weather," Brad prophecied.

Chinook reached matter of factly into the manger for a stray oat and rested her left hip, which earlier years of racing before we got her had stiffened, when Brad tied her in the Gething stable early the next morning. But Copper's soft nose prodded my pocket for sugar and after I gave it to her and to Chinook, her soft breathing cooled my open palm. They were an amiable pair. We heard Mr. Gething's already loaded wagon cramping, as his team wheeled it out of the barn.

A hush still enveloped Hudson Hope, broken only by the drone of a truck winding up the sharp switchback at the start of the portage road. The bluff there rose almost straight up from the flat with the narrow thoroughfare pinned against its incline, twisting in and out. In the open space on the high cutbank of the river, in what had been H.B.C. yard, a helicopter started its roar, rotating blades reflecting the first slant of sunlight. The team, whose feet had been fidgeting, lunged into a trot.

We passed the back of the new two-story frame hotel at the corner opposite the long closed Bay. The original, beautiful little log hotel, where Mr. and Mrs. Bob Ferguson had welcomed us the first night we'd ever slept in Hudson Hope, had burned suddenly one night a few years before. Incidentally, I was the only guest, since Brad was up the Alaska Highway with Gary and Olive Powell, hunting sheep.

A hastily formed brigade, passing pails of water from the spring just across the road, had done no good. They had continued it only to drench the roof of the upwind building next to the hotel which, otherwise, stood by itself on the pie-wedge corner. Then some of the helpless bystanders began liberating boxes of bottled beer from the bar. My diamond engagement ring and everything else I had with me, except the nightgown, robe and slippers I was wearing had burned because no one could get to that part of the building.

"Easy," Mr. Gething was saying to his team, "easy. The roan is a tartar. He's an original, you know, only half-gelded. He held back when Gene Boring did the job, but he'll be all right when we hit the hill. He's a natural trotter, but his mate Brownie, although heavy and strong, is an older mare and holds him back. Frank's line comes from the Charles E. Bedaux expedition that started out from here in 1934 with Frank Swannell, the surveyor, in charge."

"The Fergusons were telling us about it," I said. "The expedition was trying to see if a road could be put through from here to Alaska."

"That's the one," Mr. Gething said. "Mr. Bedaux's wife Fern was along. She was very regular." The cragginess of his ruggedly line face mellowed, as the shagginess of an old mountain does when warmed by the early morning sun.

He had arranged poplar saplings in eyebolts along the sides of the wagon and had stretched a ragged canvas handily across it for shade, giving us the aspect of a covered wagon. The top detailed a round blob of shadow ahead of it, while behind us, dust drawn up by the iron rims of the wheels hovered like a rolling cloud.

The small poplars and the lodgepole pines that stragggled up from the town into the endless forests had a shrunken, dry look, as if they had been burned and cut over many times. Trucks had brought in tons of gravel, but the corduroy beneath still made itself felt when we crossed the muskeg east of the new airfield. Bushman, running behind, snapped at a grasshopper, I saw that the pin cherries beside the road, light-red drupes about a quarter-inch across with their refreshing sour pulp and juice, wore a graying of dust. Mr. Gething reined to the right to let the team drink in Four-Mile Creek; I watched the resulting bubbles flock under the bridge with the current. A truck clattered over the planks.

"An International," Mr. Gething indentified it, "what the truckers hereabouts call a corn binder. Colin Campbell, who drives sometimes for King, calls his a bucket of bolts, but I notice he just bought another one and hired a second driver."

Prince lifted his dripping head and when they were back on the hard-packed ground again, he led the mare into a jolting trot, the two horses bending their necks together as if they enjoyed it. As if to share in the pleasure, Mr. Gething snapped the reins over their lathering backs.

Although we never thought of him as that, he was an old man. But his soft voice, clear gray eyes, healthily ruddy cheeks and thatch of white hair were charged with verve and strength. The fact that he was widely and profoundly read came out in his casual conversation: the talk turned somehow to early Roman times, taking Brad back to seven years of since-then scarcely used Latin.

The way Neal Gething talked was as if, just as he had something to suggest to us, no doubt we had something equally as important to tell him. It had been when he first pointed out a few of the local edible plants to us soon after we'd arrived in Hudson Hope, as if we already knew all about them, that I realized how gentle if strong he was, how simple but deep, and how with him reading was not an escape but a search. His point of view was a particularly bright hope, I was finding, in what was for Brad and me a forbidding and disillusioning period.

Much of his personality was reflected in his next-to-oldest son, the competent, unassuming, amiable and obliging King. Living day by day, King never seemed surprised and always made the best of everything, even if it were only a few minutes which he could improve by brewing a can of tea. King was also extremely knowledgeable, perhaps even more philosophical than his father; he, too, never intruded his very obvious superiority as a human being. Brad and I had always considered ourselves fortunate that the Gethings were our friends.

King had everything ready at the head of the portage. After he and we had helped Mr. Gething unload and reload his covered wagon and watched it depart in a saffron glory of dusting clay, he started the one-time automobile engine: the north bank and the old cabin started gradually to back away from the boat. For a few minutes there was the narrowing, increasingly swift current with the menace of Rocky Mountain Canyon a few hundred feet behind us. Then we were in a more placid part of the Peace River, heading upstream.

Bushman and I had already picked spots in the bow. Brad stayed behind to talk with King, who was adjusting some part of the carburetor with his slim right hand while steering with his left. I thought he looked more like a scholar than a riverman, although it was easy to see from the delicate sureness with which he handled the boat why he had early won the name the *King of the River*. He had been christened Quentin Franklin Gething.

The blue miles unfolded behind us in an ever-changing artistry of God-made splendor. Trying to embellish such pageantry with another unnecessary dam, in this age of atomic power, was like gift-wrapping a Titian.

The heavily timbered loveliness of the Canadian Rockies, which we were traversing east to west, pressed in about us on both sides of the Peace. Once we came upon a swimming Stone mountain sheep and, another time, a dog-paddling black bear. Except for the echoing roar of the built-in motor, into which thin copper tubing ran from a great red gasoline drum, we journeyed in nearly unbroken silence. I found the peacefulness welcome and deeply companionable. Whenever time seemed to lag there was King with his stories, told with one-handed gestures in a voice so unassumingly low that I had to strain my ears to hear.

It was relaxing, for even so short an interval, to break all bonds with the tension and proddings of modern-day living as it had finally come to Hudson Hope; to be transported outward in distance and backward in time from the din, the massive efficiency, the somehow savage dissatisfaction of what had become the destiny of this wildnerness. We were still heading into the sunset up the placid Peace River among the nearly untouched Rocky Mountains of northern British Columbia, but we had left civilization behind. Above and around the boat was only the moving silence of blue air and water, and peaks streaming cloud that looked like volcano smoke, all confirming the vivid watercolors of local artist Michael John Richmond.

The only other signs of our fellow man—unless you counted the very occasional trapper's cabin, usually in the angle between a crystalline stream and the murky river—was a huge freight canoe with a tremendous outboard operated by a steersman in an elevated chair above the stern. Everyone waved as they passed.

"Dick Corliss," King said. "He's headed downriver, probably for the last time, to fill up with vegetables from Mrs. Beattie's garden at Gold Bar."

Day succeeded day, full of mountain-bounded space and peace and the throbbing of an old automobile motor, each twenty-four hours as nearly alike as the hand-crafted turquoises of a Navajo necklace. Occasionally, when we wanted a change of diet, we'd stop to fish at the mouth of one of the streams. Casting our black gnats and brown hackles where the clear current met the silt-laden Peace, we landed a rainbow trout or Arctic grayling on the average of every other throw.

King was never in a hurry but sometimes, when the shore was mountainous and bare, we'd cook our catch on the portable sheet-iron Sims stove that he'd had set up on a gravel-filled box in the bow. I usually wielded the great frypan to which he'd attached a long, cool wooden handle. King could always improvise. One morning, after we'd arrived at our camping place too late the night before to bother to unpack more than our sleeping bags and air mattresses, he built a roaring fire on the beach. He scoured the flat black scoop of a new prospector's shovel with sand and fried our bacon and eggs in that, the lengthy handle being a convenience as it allowed him to stand well away from the heat.

King told us how, during the great depression of the Thirties, there had been gravel punchers on nearly every creek and bar, panning wages. He had delivered the mail then. He'd bought supplies for many of the prospectors, too; they'd got others at the trading post at Finlay Forks, also soon to be deep under water. As he spoke, his dark osprey eyes, framed by long lashes and the black stubble of several days, became as lustrous as the Peace's surface.

"Especially up on the headwaters, this Peace River country is rich with gold," he said now, "and gold, as soon as it is out from under government control, will be worth nine times or more what it was selling for when the Klondike Stampede passed through here. The lake will wipe out the gravel bars, but it will make for easier transportation to the lode claims. I have a few myself. But I hate to think of people pouring in and ruining one of the last expanses of unmapped and largely unexplored wildernesses in the world."

"That's exactly how it was marked on the first government maps we got of this region," Brad said, " 'Unmapped and Unexplored.' "

"When you come right down to it, what is money?" King said, and he lifted a hand in silent greeting to an Indian and what looked like his entire family. Having beached their large canoe, they were camped on shore. "Probably came down the Crooked River from Summit Lake outside of Prince George . . . . To get back to money; there's money to be made in other parts of the world. But there's only so much wilderness and when that's gone, it's gone forever. Wasn't it your Daniel Webster who said, 'There's nothing so powerful as truth, and often nothing so strange'?"

The blueness was flowing out of the sky and the river, as if it were seeping through a hidden hole in the mountains. A full moon climbed behind us, adding its gold to the turbulent crimsons, yellows, and the more somber Tyrian purple of the sunset. The colors struck gauntness to a forlorn and stunted line of evergreens, up where the timberline was silhouetted against the distance.

We cruised on through the twilight of pale amber. The breeze that had quieted with this perceptible blending of the past and the future began to stir again, balmily but with a shrillness between the cutbanks. Time was no more than the evanescent gleam of the two hands of Brad's wristwatch, shimmering above the dim incandescence of the numerals.

Intervening leaves, now that I glanced back, were making the moon a shivering Chinese gong. Little ripples humped against either side of the pointed bow, spacing themselves on the quiet water into parallel lines that stretched behind us in the moonlight until they broke like jewels against each shore.

"Selwyn is that high mountain just up ahead to the left," King said. To my ears, his words had an almost dreamlike quality.

Never before in my life, I thought, had I seen such a keenly outlined and textured mass of green. Topped by gleaming and glossy white, these slopes and ridges and spires appeared to be drifting very gradually toward us in a dark-polished sky, so brilliant a blue that it might have been the heart of a flame. This height seemed to be calling to us even more than its brother Bullhead at the other side of the range, soaring as it did into the silence of chilled, glimmering, colorless, cloud-scoured space. I was only sorry that the shadows of evening were already reaching higher and higher on its lower inclines, lifting directly from the south shore.

"We'll camp across the way on the Wicked River," King said now, as if reading my thoughts. A slow smile creased his long intelligent face, rusted by the weather. "You two can get an early start in the morning. There's some iron outcroppings I want to investigate for the next couple of days, at least, up the Wicked, so you may as well take your time. I'll be coming back to camp each night, so just build a fire on the opposite shore whenever you want me to come over in the boat and pick you up."

23

Mountain of Gold

We climbed through a steep slant of spruce first, then there was a path of sorts heading generally east and upward, where the dream-lightened boots of early prospectors had furrowed this Mountain of Gold. The trail rose and dropped, ascended again, fell once more, yet always it lifted to a spot a bit loftier than before.

The wide, fleece-padded straps of a small contour packsack carrying my mummy bag and a few personal possessions cut into my shoulders, although that was all right. Ahead of me Brad was carrying the light mountain tent in addition to his own sleeping bag, on a packboard that he'd built from an Alaskan model. Brad's book, *Wilderness Gear You Can Make Yourself*, shows how it's done.

Bushman, bringing the few cooking and eating supplies, was ahead, behind, all over; as filled with quiet exultation, apparently, as I was. Matching Brad's easy stride, I felt the first weariness at the steepness of the ascent flowing out of my muscles, replaced with a profound and fathomless conviction of happiness at being here on such a day, in such company, and climbing.

The gradient became so steep that, when we stopped in midmorning and surveyed where we had been, the Wicked River was a mere silver thread far below. The trappers' cabin in the clearing on the eastern edge of the river's stone-flecked mouth was barely distinguishable. I looked ahead again and up, using our binoculars. Through the green mist of shade, silhouetted atop a ridge well above timberline, were several strangely head-heavy shapes. They were the color of the rocks, but they were moving.

"Stone mountain sheep," Brad identified. "Rams. Ready to go on?"

I was.

"Not good to rest for more than five minutes at a time." He squinted upward. "Stiffen up otherwise. Pack not too heavy?"

It wasn't.

There was only the occasional clatter of rock underfoot, the robust rhythm of our breathing, and a quiet shush of wind bearing the distant roar of what I supposed was the fast water just below Finlay Forks. Along with the brief turbulence of what the sourdoughs called Parlez Pas—because there was no sound to warn the unwary boatman coming downriver—it was one of the only two rapids in the entire breadth of the continent's backbone as far down as Rocky Mountain Canyon. It was as if I were listening to the earth twirling on its poles.

Still, always, there was pattern and significance and an immense, hidden, purposeful harmony. I had known that much even during my first girlhood dancing lessons and, later, in following the demanding, exacting grace of ballet. It wasn't something you could own or clasp, but a fervor that arrived somewhere deep within you as it had during our ordinary everyday serenity in our first log cabin and in our present one above the ledge.

You listened to it in the arias of some operas and the sentences of some prose. Even in the designed clamor of a freighter foghorn in the blackness—like the one aboard the Oriental Rio on that world cruise we had snatched during a half year away from the wilderness, after a book had sold well. You looked at it in Brad's ice-blue eyes, heard it in his portable typewriter, felt it in the crackling warmth of a lone glowing campfire.

I had glimpsed it and listened to it and sensed it as I gazed up at Bullhead Mountain, rearing like an enormous and kindly guardian above Hudson Hope, which its flanks sheltered—and now to a lesser degree, perhaps because it was a stranger to me, in the higher, more imposing, gold-rich Mount Selwyn.

Not until I bumped into him did I realize that Brad had stopped. Drinking the way he always did from a running stream, as if it were snow, Bushman was snatching mouthfuls of water from a tiny watercourse that hurried down the side of the mountain.

"I'm not really thirsty," I said.

"Good place to wash our feet and socks, anyway," Brad said. "Our feet are the most important things today. The socks will dry on the outsides of our packs. You brought spares?"

"Oh, yes," I said. "I don't think I forgot anything."

"Here's my soap," he offered.

There was the burning, biting violence of the frothing coldness against my toes, soles and, finally, my ankles, then the sharpness of rocks against my feet until I could find a boulder on which to sit and apply the small square of terry cloth toweling that I accepted gratefully. Slowly, delectably, feeling returned. Then my feet were encased in warm, fresh woolens, so soft that they seemed to have a built-in bounce to them.

"Uumm," I said. "That was good."

"Let me help you back on with your pack."

I followed the line of his gaze, slitted against the blinding brightness, to where a thin white dome lifted, dazzling and pristine, into a trailing scarf of mist.

"Is that where we're going?" I asked.

I guess I smiled so cockily that he couldn't help grinning back.

"That's it," he said, "but not before lunch. And we'd better eat before we get above timberline."

The trees were becoming sparser as we climbed, but then we came close to some ptarmigan, their brown plumage already specked with winter white. Brad, while I held Bushman, secured two of them with well-aimed rocks. He plucked and dressed them while I kindled a small hot fire in a hollow with the contorted, stunted pine that had replaced the spruce forest. Then I cut green willow branches for the roasting. Soon, hot smoky drumsticks were easing my hunger.

The short green needles of a patch of juniper, their stiffness bristling warmly through my clothes, were springy beneath me. All around, I noticed how browning pallid moss, interspersed with gray rocks and gravel and an occasional white vein of quartz, was taking the place of the dew-enchanted grass. Nearby, an old and weathered prospector's stake was a reminder of how, during the hungry Thirties, gold-seekers—whom the sourdoughs called gravel punchers—had hopefully swarmed here. After bracing black tea, Brad extinguished the fire with water from the brook and we climbed on.

"Want to lead for awhile, Vena?" he asked. "Then you can set your own pace."

"This is fine," I said, shaking my head. "It's easier when I don't have to think about where to go."

"You're not getting too tired?"

"No," I said and smiled. "You're not leaving me behind unless you hurry a whole lot faster than you've been going."

"There's no hurry," he said, "that is, if those clouds don't mean something. Isn't all this magnificent?"

Selwyn, I was finding, was more than a height of rock and snow. It was a mass of brightness and shade, unchanged since the first Indians had paddled past, yet its mien was mutative almost from minute to minute. Its image was never identical yet it was changeless, always in transition but still selfsame.

The angle of ascent sharpened. Bushman, stopping his ceaseless forays, followed us silently except for the occasional rasp of claws or the shift of shale underfoot. He seemed to be limping, but when I touched his rough gray head encouragingly, his torso, then his loins, and finally his great long tail, flailed into motion. Wind heaved below us, although here the air was still. The kyah of a gliding, occasionally wing-shifting, golden eagle pierced the silence.

"What are those mountains to the west?" I asked, as we paused on the lip of a precipice.

"King told me they're the Wolverines," he said. It seemed as if my eyes were following them into the blue distances almost as far as the headwaters of the Finlay River, which got its remote start from feeder streams just below the Yukon Territory. "Did you ever see so many glaciers?"

The glittering ice specks shone among jutting, hurtling, sprawling crags and spires and snowy towers in every direction, especially toward the north where there were a thousand snowy peaks that no man's footprints had ever marked. Toward the east, then downriver, was a confounding jumble of blue and white contours ending, although I could not pick it out, with Bullhead. The new maps called it Portage Mountain, just as they were now naming Hudson Hope Hudson's Hope, although the post office and the new branch of the Canadian Imperial Bank of Commerce still held to the old spelling.

"King says there's a lake back inland here a way." The stillness seemed to be catching, but when his eyes found mine, his broad mouth curved, and he said, "I don't know about you, but I'm hot enough to go for a swim."

"Whatever you do," I said, "I want to do, too."

We found it beneath the blazing sun in a little hollow and, with a whoop, threw off our clothing. The water, covering about half an acre, was no more than waist deep, but we managed a few strokes. The perpetual snowbank from which it was fed was reflected in silk-smooth water; around it, nearby crags made perpendiculars as sharp as opalescent minarets. I suddenly felt as exotic as Scheherazade.

The water, if burning cold, was as invigorating as a slow caress. Then a pitchfork of lightning heaved the clouds apart, followed by another and another.

"We'd better get out of here," Brad said. The next instant, we were in our boots and, clothing in hand, running toward a good-sized gravity cave up a slight slope. "That should be safe."

The cave was shallow, if high, and I made out the tracks of mountain sheep at its broad mouth, as I felt the vigor returning like fire through the muscles and marrows of my exhausted body.

The thunderheads were gone as quickly as they had massed, lightning still pronging their dark underbellies. Except for an occasional distant rumble, I could feel the hush in the atmosphere. The lake sprawled below like a dim mirror. Some birds I didn't recognize were swooping low over it, filling the silence with their twitterings. Then it began to snow, heavily, blindingly, and the thin air was abruptly more bitterly cold than we were dressed for.

"No fuel up here," Brad said tersely. "We'd better get down to timberline while we can build a campfire and put up the tent."

The radiant day had died young and the heavens were in mourning for it, although enough light filtered through erratic gaps in the clouds to emphasize that the darkness was premature. Snow was everywhere, even invading the open cave with the suffocating whiteness with which train smoke envelops a tunnel; as if it were the steaming breath of a prehistoric wyvern. Visibility was for the time being smothered as effectively as if we were being blanketed with raw cotton.

"Keep close and watch your feet," Brad was saying. "Luckily, I always carry a compass. Where's Bushman?"

"He's right behind me," I said. "He keeps walking on my heels."

Great cold flakes buffeted us in horizontal fury, while the

tumult swooped at us from every direction in a sort of fervored turbulence, as if it were attempting to whip the last shreds of life from the condemned wilderness. It had been such a golden afternoon, wonderful, windless, that I could scarcely credit that the universe was now whirling with tempest.

"Let me cut one of these long willow switches," Brad said, halting so suddenly that I collided with him. "Then I can feel ahead so that we won't be walking off a cliff."

The wind rose even higher, like a surf whose waves were blinding, stinging, freezing snow. We furrowed through it, going downward more steeply now into the storm that, like an enormous pennant, unfurled up the slope in a twisting, cavorting rush. I felt as exposed as if I were standing on a low-fenced captain's walk atop one of Portsmouth, New Hampshire's seashore mansions in an New England hurricane.

Then, as we reached the first straggling, runty pines, the snow and the wind ceased as abruptly as they had started. For two or three minutes, there were a few stinging pellets of sleet, then the odd drop of rain, then nothing. For awhile, as we hiked lower, the ground was wet and slippery underfoot; then, when the first spruce appeared, it was as dusty underfoot as it had been when we climbed up. I counted seven separate rainbows and we even walked through the arch of one; a brilliant blend of colors, then the dullness of nothingness in its midst and, finally, the ordered beauty of the curving hues once more. In the depths below, the remaining daylight became virescent, then azure as it dimmed to a dreamlike dusk.

"What about camping here for the night?" Brad asked near the edge of a precipice, his deep voice pleasantly disturbing my reveries. "There's flatness, water, fuel and even a view."

"I'm just glad we don't walk in our sleep," I said.

"It's all right then, Vena?" he grinned.

"It's fine, Brad," I said, smiling in return. "If you'll solve the intricacies of that little mountain tent, I'll get in the firewood."

"You," he said, "have yourself a deal. Even with clearing the ground, I'll have it up before you're finished. It's compact, that's all, not really complicated."

The tent proved to be green and inviting with the last of the sun on it. The atmosphere inside appeared to have the vitality of a living lake, as if the soft grass were shining up through the thin floor. The prevailing breezes from the west were just vigorous enough to heave slight swells in the nylon sides, which seemed less synthetic covering than leafy canopy as they bellied and sagged, appearing to catch handfuls of the sunlight and then to drain them off, as though the ebbing radiance were a sudden fall shower.

Brad had had the shelter especially made with a small canopy in front that he now propped wide with two slanting poles. He built the small glowing campfire just beyond its edge. It was a small enchanted world with the verdant shade of the nylon, the mountain grass under the fabric, the rustling lodgepole pines outside and the soft whisper of breezes that enveloped us. My spine was tingling strangely. Never before, not even while dancing "Swan Lake," had I sensed such freshness and sharpness in the air.

"I wonder what Alaska would be like?" I said as we toasted our cheese sandwiches.

"Whenever it opens up, it'll be the richest of all," Brad reflected. "But we'd pretty much have to be on the spot to take advantage of the land sales. That would be expensive and might take a long time."

"Well," I said, "there's the Atlin here in British Columbia; we were thinking about it before.

"I guess you were up in the bow when I was talking with King about the Atlin. He says it looks as if a new provincial government is going to come into power here in B.C., and they'll no longer even lease crown land to Americans. Not only that, but they're going to stop transferring land to anyone at all unless a road already leads there."

"Roads again," I said disconsolately. "Isn't there some wilderness left somewhere?"

"Well," he waved an arm toward the rich and radiant glaciers that glowed in such shades of lustrous grandeur that they lit up the sweeping expanse of northern sky. "Right in between Alaska and British Columbia there's the glorious Yukon.

24

The Glorious Yukon

Back at the turn of the century, when a bunch of the boys were whooping it up at the Malemute Saloon, the Yukon had by far its greatest population. Some of the cabins of those early trappers and prospectors are still standing. In recent years, too, people have begun to move into the larger settlements, leaving many isolated homes deserted. In today's crowded world, these often afford empty space, peace and quiet.

Fur was the initial attraction to the vast Yukon wilderness. Gold quickly displaced it. Although the presence of the yellow metal was known earlier from the finds in Alaska, it was not until 1873 that prospectors began arriving in numbers. Many of the earlier arrivals, some of whom were sufficiently beguiled by the land to stay, came from California where the strike of '49 had passed. Some entered the Yukon from the north, up the still important Yukon River from Alaska. Others, swarming in from the south, were the first to cross Chilkoot Pass from Alaska's port town of Skagway in 1884.

When in August 1896, the famous Klondike strike made its still visible history, thousands of Americans and others poured into the region. Dawson, at the meeting of the Klondike and Yukon Rivers, became a city of 25,000. Some of the old cabins still stand and a couple who were lured north from New York by Brad's books recently wrote us that they've just occupied one. By 1910, the Yukon's total population had fallen to 8512; ghost towns and camps remain to this day.

The present population is roughly 21,000. A breakdown shows

that the average age of inhabitants is twenty-seven years, indicating that the young look to the Territory as a country of opportunity and challenge. There is also the fascination of being a part of the history of the Yukon, still very much in the making.

There is still only one Dawson City, however: the scene of the most fantastic gold rush the world has ever witnessed. On 17 August 1896, George Carmack, along with his Indian companions Tagish Charlie and Skookum Jim, scooped nuggets out of a stream eleven miles from Dawson and named it Bonanza. From that electrifying moment, Bonanza, Eldorado and the Klondike became known throughout the world.

One of the meanings of the Indian name Yukon is *greatest river* while Klondike is the Indian cognomen for *hammerwater*, so called because stakes were hammered into the stream to trap the salmon. Though only 180 miles south of the Arctic Circle, Dawson became known as the Paris of the North, with elaborate hotels, theaters and dance halls rivaling those of San Francisco. To the sound of honky-tonk pianos, roulette wheels, church bells and boat whistles, enough gold came out of the valleys in bulging pokes and on pack horses to turn a few pick-and-shovel miners into free-spending millionaires. Many a valuable claim was passed over, too.

Land of legend and derring-do, where in the summer the sun never sets, the Yukon with its lofty mountains, snow-white glaciers, birch-clad valleys and sparkling myriads of silent lakes is prime log cabin country.

Mount Logan, which soars 19,850 feet in the southwestern part of the Territory, is Canada's loftiest mountain and second only in North America to Alaska's Mt. McKinley. A major topographic feature of the Yukon, however, is the basinlike region known as the Yukon Plateau. These rolling uplands in the interior have an average elevation of 2000 to 3000 feet and are almost completely surrounded by peaks.

White spruce, slender lodgepole pine, balsam, poplar, white birch which the Indians use for snowshow frames, black spruce and tamarac are found in that portion of Canada's boreal forest region which covers the Yukon Territory. There are prime log cabin materials. Because of the latitude and altitude, however, much of the best forest area is limited to major valleys. The timberline varies from about 5000 feet above sea level in the south to about 4000 feet and less at latitude 65° North.

Wild flowers grow in great abundance almost everywhere in the Yukon, and anyone who goes up there should have some good books on edible wild plants with him. A couple of Brad's are mentioned earlier; some other good ones are O. P. Medsger's *Edible Wild Plants* and Michael Weiner's *Earth Medicine-Earth Foods*. Nearly 500 varieties of flowers, shrubs and ferns have been identified. They are most profuse in the valleys and on the lower slopes, although they are found even in the higher areas above timberline. Characteristic species include the North's striking and savory fireweed, which is the Yukon's floral emblem; arnica daisies, which can be used to make the well-known tincture; scrubby cinquefoil; marsh marigold, the yellow pond lily so relished by moose; yellow violet; and the bright arctic poppy.

Glacier-fed lakes and magnificent mountains combine in the Yukon to create breathtaking views that are equal to any in the world. Visitors and new settlers like to see Robert W. Service's old cabin in Dawson and the one reputed to have belonged to Sam McGee, who was cremated at nearby Lake Lebarge: the structure has been moved as a museum to the center of Whitehorse. A few miles away is lofty Miles Canyon, where Jack London earned a living as a river pilot before heading for the northern gold fields.

A heady feeling of wilderness freedom awaits the outdoor lover who travels the engineering epic known as the Alaska Highway to Canada's Yukon Territory, larger than California and Pennsylvania combined. Thousands of soldiers and civilians, armed with giant road-building machines, carved the 1523-mile thoroughfare out of British Columbia, Yukon and Alaska wilderness during the critical days of World War II. Today the road north is an artery of commerce, as well as a path to excitement, adventure and rip-roaring history for the whole family—be they sportsmen, rockhounds, bird watchers or amateur photographers. You can enjoy other hobbies, too.

The glittering ice that sheathed most of northern Canada during the last Ice Age was in retreat some 30,000 years ago; it is quite possible that the first Canadians came from Asia via Alaska soon after the ice began to recede. This conjecture is substantiated by the fact that a very large part of the Yukon River drainage—a vast central basin in the heart of the Yukon Territory and Alaska—was never glaciated and was therefore likely fit for human habitation during the latter part of the Ice Age. Artifacts are still being found in quantity in the Yukon, the earliest so far being some 7000 years old. There's also valuable mastodon ivory.

With a throaty roar from her shiny brass whistle, on 17 July 1897 the North American Trading and Transportation Company's Alaska steamer *Portland* eased into Seattle. Hanging over the rails and generally whooping it up sourdough-style, was a group of Klondike miners loaded with fresh gold from the creeks. They had it stuffed in jam tins, Bull Durham tobacco sacks and foot-long moosehide pokes.

William Stanley of Seattle carried $112,000 in gold dust. One P. Weare owned $177,500 in the yellow metal, deposited with the ship's purser. Thomas Moran of Montreal staggered ashore with another $20,000 of flour gold and nuggets. Over a million dollars worth of gleaming tawny metal was hidden in the dark corners of the vessel. Newspaper headlines inspired the call of "Let's go!" in the minds of thousands. It is estimated by our friend Roy Minter, longtime assistant to the president of the White Pass & Yukon Route, that over 100,000 individuals swarmed through Dawson alone at the height of the rush.

Mining is still the Yukon's foremost industry, although lead and zinc have replaced gold in importance, with copper, silver and asbestos following. Platinum, tungsten, cadmium and coal are also to be found. Oil and gas exploration, receiving further impetus from the discoveries on Alaska's North Slope, is increasing. The proximity of the Japanese market with its scarcity of raw materials, abundance of productive facilities, technological skill and capital is of growing importance in the Yukon, where claim-staking activity has risen spectacularly.

Any individual over eighteen years of age has the right, with a few reservations, to prospect and mine upon lands in the Yukon Territory where the right to dig minerals has not yet been alienated from the Crown. The fee for recording a claim is $10. However, it costs nothing to look.

Copies of the Yukon Quartz and Placer Mining Acts and other mining regulations may be obtained from the Mining Recorders at Whitehorse, Dawson, Watson Lake and Mayo, as well as from the Resources Division, Indian and Northern Affairs, Ottawa, Ontario.

Would you like to have your own falcon? The Yukon is a prime nesting area for several species of these notable hunting birds. Be sure not to plunder any of the endangered types though.

Spectacular Dall sheep range southward to the Ogilvie Mountains and the Saint Elias Range, intermingling in the central Yukon with the much desired Stone sheep. Mountain goats are common in the Saint Elias Range and across the southern portion of the Territory. Huge moose, rivaled only by those in Alaska and in northwestern British Columbia, range north as far as the MacMillan River and Ogilvie Mountains and the Porcupine-Yukon boundaries area. Grizzly and black bear are found in the interior, the former measuring up to eight feet in length.

Barren ground caribou migrate across the land in vast river-swimming herds. There are also ptarmigan, which change their plumage with the seasons, five varieties of grouse and abundant waterfowl. Wolves, coyotes, wolverine and cougar may be shot at any time. Fur-bearers include the industrious beaver, ebony-tipped ermine, mink, marten, the valuable fisher, muskrat, rollicking otter, softly padding lynx and the warmly coated Arctic fox. All in all, Yukon hunting is among the best on the continent.

Residents may purchase a general hunting license for $5. A resident trapping license also costs $5; game birds, $4. The big game and game bird license for nonresident Canadians and other British subjects is $50, for aliens $100. However, nonresidents can stay happy on roast ptarmigan, grilled grouse and such for a $15 license. There are also guide requirements until you're a qualified resident. Further particulars are available from the Director of Game, Box 2703, Whitehorse, Yukon Territory.

There is no closed season for sport fishing in the Yukon, where you can live high twelve months a year on Arctic grayling, lake trout, Dolly Varden, landlocked salmon, cutthroat trout, rainbow, steelhead, king and Chinook salmon, soho salmon and the fighting northern pike. Once you're a Canadian resident, a license is but $3, while for nonresidents it's only $10. While you're looking over the country, you may fish in the Territory for five days for $3.50. No licenses are necessary for anyone under sixteen. For further details write the Fisheries Services, 1100A First Avenue, Whitehorse, Yukon Territory.

When you're a Canadian citizen or have served in the Canadian Armed Forces and want large amounts of fish to dry for your personal use and for your dogs, you may get a $25 commerical license to use a gill net and to set up a fish-wheel. If you're on the Yukon River downstream from Dawson, by the way, you can use that fish-wheel for catching delectable quantities of salmon.

The Yukon Territory, which many assert gets its name from the Indian word *yuckoo*, meaning clear water, extends norhtward from British Columbia to the Arctic Ocean and eastward from Alaska to the Northwest Territories. Two thirds of this area ranges between 2000 and 5000 feet above sea level, with 4000 to 8000 foot mountains comprising most of the remainder. The climate at these altitudes is bracing, with most of the limited precipitation fortunately falling from June to October.

The long-term average January temperatures are similar to those in the thriving city of Winnipeg, Manitoba. The frost, which is stimulating rather than enervating or disagreeable, shouldn't keep anyone home. All in all, the Yukon is still a haven for the hearty.

Yukon summers are warm with restfully cool nights. Rainfall is very light and generally of short duration. The humidity is low, producing, in harmony with the clear air, a healthful invigorating climate. Lengthy winter nights are offset by long summer days, twenty-four hours of daylight occurring in some parts of this Land of the Midnight Sun.

Generally speaking, all Yukon lakes and the great Yukon River, with its numerous tributaries, are navigable from the time of the spring breakup until the fall freeze, roughly May to October. River currents, varying from two to five miles per hour, provide engrossing downhill runs. None of the waterways mentioned is often plagued by any death-defying aspects, but inasmuch as these routes wend through practically uninhabited wilderness, you should expect to be self-sufficient. Incidentally, when you're fishing or exploring you need have no worries about snakes, poison ivy or the noisome poison oak.

Hot springs bubble out of the ground in the vicinity of the Toad River Gorge, some of my favorite Yukon country, near the Liard River nearly 500 miles north of the Alaska Highway's Mile 0 at Dawson Creek.

The winters vary. On New Year's Day in 1970, for example, a dozen canoeists raced down the open Yukon River at Whitehorse for a full mile, just for the fun of it. It was a balmy 40° above, and more than 2000 sourdoughs turned out in the bright, warm sunshine to watch the sport.

On the other hand, it was a rousing 81° below at Snag back in 1947. Put this up against record summer heat of 97° above in Mayo and 94.2° in Whitehorse, comparable to anything you'll find in the more southern climes of the Dominion. Inhabitants of the Yukon don't worry too much about the extremely high and drastically low temperatures that sometimes arrive, because they happen so seldom. They just enjoy all those beautiful temperatures in between.

Crown land is available to live on in the Yukon, although surveyors are now a couple of years behind in mapping it, but not ordinarily for easy speculation. Leases and agreements of sale, based on the reasonably low appraised values, contain clauses requiring you to make certain improvements within two years and to occupy the property until these have been made. After that, of course, you can sell out, but most prefer to stay. A surprising and always heartening number of refugees from U.S. cities, on their way to a new freedom in the Yukon Territory, make the trip in to Hudson Hope some fifty miles west off the Alaska Highway to talk with us about the possibilities.

An individual wishing to acquire Territorial land must select the parcel that seems best suited to his requirements; the best way to do this is to visit the Yukon. The Department of Northern Affairs and National Resources maintains Land Offices at Whitehorse, Mayo, Dawson and Watson Lake. The Land Agents in these outposts are generally well qualified and are always willing to assist an applicant in the selection of his cabin site.

In recent years there has been a general exodus of the population to the centers of civilization and at the moment—with government surveyors so far behind—the best bet for Americans wishing to take to the woods is personally to seek out people who are moving. Buy privately, without the inflation of a real estate dealer, a cabin or homestead in the area that most appeals to you. There are plenty of choices, but *always* see the property yourself before making the final purchase!

Of the 21,000 people in the Yukon, there's a sizable preponderance of males, an imbalance not unusual in a frontier area. About 13,000 of these people live in Whitehorse. The second most populous community is Faro (about 1500), while the major part of the remaining population is divided among Dawson, Watson Lake, Haines Junction and Mayo. The 207,076 square miles of land in the Yukon Territory provide nearly a dozen square miles of elbow room for each inhabitant.

Always interesting neighbors, less than 3000 Indians—belonging to the Athabaskan language group—now inhabit the Yukon. In the northern half of the Territory, the Loucheux operate fishwheels and fish traps, while in the southern half are the colorful Tagish, Slave, Tlingit, Nahanee, Kutchin and Sicanee.

In 1942, during the construction of the Alaska Highway, many Indians in the southeastern and western Yukon had their first contact with modern civilization. Now it is a common sight to see Indians operating the mammoth earth-moving machinery that once terrified their parents. Hunting, trapping and fishing presently supplement the Indians' income from construction, mining, handicrafts, highway maintenance, guiding and various other trades. Maybe you'll be able to hire one to help you with your log cabin.

Trucking services are well developed on the Alaska Highway. Truckers operating within the Yukon itself carry about 750,000 tons of freight yearly, much of it the product of the mines. The enterprising White Pass & Yukon Route's narrow-gauge railroad, connecting with the Alaskan coast, is the principal means of moving freight to and from the Yukon, with considerably greater tonnages going south than coming into the north.

Restored sternwheelers, some of which may still be seen in Whitehorse, Dawson and Carcross, once plied the Yukon River between Whitehorse and Dawson; however, except for scattered craft and mining-company river boats and chartered barges still on the Yukon and Porcupine, local transportation is now almost entirely handled by the expanding road system.

Canadian Coachways provides modern bus transportation, with regular service from points in British Columbia and northern Alberta. It supplies international connections to all parts of the continent, including Alaska. Taxis and car rental agencies operate in all larger communities. Air transportation is especially important, airports and landing strips being located throughout the Territory.

The country is being opened by a greatly increased road-building program, doubling that of even the past decade. All potential areas of resource development are being brought to within 200 miles of some permanent highway. Road construction is continuing on two routes. The Dempster Highway, which will eventually connect Dawson with Fort MacPherson and the MacKenzie Delta of the Northwest Territories, is nearing the Arctic Circle. And in the southern Yukon, work is progressing on the Skagway to Carcross road. Besides making the wilderness more readily available to log cabin seekers, these efforts are also reducing the dependence on seasonal transportation and thus reducing costs.

Schools in the Yukon go to the university-entrance level. An estimated 5000 students presently attend twenty-two public and

Roman Catholic schools in the Territory. Then there's the preemployment education to be gained at the Yukon Vocational and Technical Training Center in Whitehorse, where two modern hostels accommodate students from rural areas.

Suppose your youngsters live far out in the bush? They can avail themselves of the fine educational facilities provided by the government in a tie-in with British Columbia's wealth of correspondence courses.

In addition to answering a continuing high demand for general library services, the Regional Library in Whitehorse, which serves sixty-eight different outlets, is now providing a centralized service of fully catalogued books for school libraries. And here there's time to read.

25

Tent on Mount Selwyn

A strange thing about the wind was how it eased out of the tent. The thin nylon, poplar-green in the small crackling glow of the campfire, appeared somehow to leak atmosphere outward. I could nearly feel the ponderousness of the mountain-clinging drafts on the fabric above and about me. With a snap, the pine-laden air would draw in from below the zippered opening in front like an inhalation, expanding the hollows before it was slowly sucked out once more, until I had the giddy sensation of lying in a vacuum.

I finally gave up fighting insomnia and wriggled out of my mummy bag as quietly as I could in the cramped quarters so as not to disturb the still deeply breathing Brad. I took my down jacket and boots, for otherwise I had slept fully clothed, and went out to join Bushman by the fire. Soon he was stretching happily, too, flailing his long dark tail, nuzzling me as I eased fresh fuel onto the glowing yellow lantern of the embers.

The Big and Little Dippers, Orion, Cassiopeia—and what seemed to be most of the other approximately two thousand stars that can be seen by the unaided eye—burned in the brilliance of the night. The lacquered blackness was diminished only slightly by a faint fluttering of Northern Lights and what was left of an horizon-margined moon. Between them and Selwyn a pervasive presence of air, so faint that it nearly expired on the very rim of sensation, persisted from the west like a fourth companion on the mountain.

"Hi, honey."

It was Brad, fully dressed, and he went to plunge his face and hands into the nearby brook before sitting with me in the flickerings of the campfire. He drew my head onto his down-softened shoulder and, although he didn't speak, his warmth and strength told all there was to say of his loneliness, his doubts and fears.

"Hungry?" I asked.

"Well . . . ." He turned with an entranced expression to breathe in the gentle dawn breeze that was wafting eastward across the headwaters of the Peace. It brought with it the incense of lodgepole pines, ideal for cabin building, that I had seen thriving during our trips to Whitehorse and from there across the mountains to Skagway on the Alaskan coast.

"I didn't think we'd want to forage for breakfast, especially if we got up in the dark. So I brought some bannock makings, tiger and dried eggs."

"Tiger," he translated with a laugh. "I take it you're quoting our friend Dudley. Dud always says that bacon, being striped, sounds nobler when called tiger; I guess he's right."

"Will you put on the tea pail," I asked, "while I'm starting the tiger, the way it should be, over a few coals in a cold frypan? Then the grease will give some flavor to the dehydrated eggs. I brought along a package of flour, baking powder and salt: I'll mix it into a fairly stiff dough with a little brook water, then ribbon it on a green stick for you to hold."

"We're in business," he said, giving me a kiss while rising to his feet. "Don't worry about Bush. He'll soon have all the rabbit he can eat."

The Aurora Borealis had bannered even lower over the great

valley eroded by the Peace River; now it fluttered a wavering silver thread over the meandering stream. The cutbanks below, with the forest blackening their very edges, scissored the water with heavy shadows which, here and there, snipped the reflection of the celestial radiance.

A conifer-perfumed breeze, like the smell of moonlight, was strengthening in the west from Finlay Forks. The moon-filled clouds were pressing from the remains of that body. Behind us, especially with its flap open, the tent was whipping and snapping with increasing jerks. Otherwise we ate in silence, listening to the increasing wind screaming in the guy ropes, then sweeping on in resonant, unfettered music up the dark sparseness beyond timberline. It quieted again with the coming of the gray dawn.

"Do you remember that day when we first learned we'd have to leave our original home site?" my husband asked, as if swept along with memories.

"Yes, Brad."

"And being caught not long after in that snowslide up near Starfish Creek? I might never have reached you in time if it hadn't been for Bushman."

I nodded.

"And the grizzly at our winter's meat? And the night we drove the wolf pack away from that moose they'd brought down?"

"Yes."

"And our ride to town for the mail during that cold spell? And the candle ice up above Box Canyon? And that wild run down the river when we first built The Peacemaker?"

"How could I ever forget that?"

"And the bull moose we cornered up Starfish Creek? The four grizzlies? And wondering whether we should go to Hollywood?"

"Oh, yes."

"After all these years in Hudson Hope—nearly twenty-five of them—do you want to keep on trying to stay for as long as we can? And if we finally have to move to the Yukon, always to keep a home here?"

He hesitated and stared at me in the firelight and was about to continue, but then all of a sudden he realized there was no need to say anything more. My face was tear-shined and my hands, in his, were quivering and holding on with all their might.

"Oh, yes, Brad," I heard myself saying eagerly, earnestly, almost desperately. "Yes, yes!"

Arguments in the outside world were becoming more irate, I knew: walls were higher and the shadow of mushroom clouds was drifting ominously over great nations and small alike. But the wilderness, sustaining and ever filled with fresh life, still held us with silken bonds. And who could tell? Perhaps in the holocaust to come, it might be overlooked. We'd had the best of it here and now to the north, in case we ever had to leave our sanctuary in Rocky Mountain Canyon, there was other wilderness.

I repeated to myself the sentences of Brad's invitation to return to show business, advertising, and publishing, but they were only sentences, relating to an obscure and nearly forgotten city nightmare which no longer had reality or substance.

Reality now was the blue, slanting river and the ledge above the river; the cabin above the ledge and the foothills of the Canadian Rockies above the cabin. Reality was Brad walking slowly and silently through the Far Northern muskegs and the forests and the mountains, and my following surely beside him. There was still enough of the true, the good, and the beautiful in the world, I realized, if one had but the steadfastness to hold onto them.

"We're staying!" he exulted.

He laughed. After a moment I joined in, but my laughter turned to happy tears. Then all of a sudden we were in each other's arms, clinging as though some *force majeure* were trying to wrench us apart.

Forever is tomorrow, I thought, but it's yesterday, too. It was almost as if we were walking together to the world's ending.

Taking the binoculars, I looked down at the mouth of the Wicked River on the other side of the Peace.

"King is here," I said. "He's by his boat, still fishing."

By subtle degrees, the darkness was beginning to lighten. A wave of radiance poured down the mountainside, like a lustrous liquid into an enormous trough, and touching their heights was the sun, lifting colossal and golden above the peaks downriver. What seemed to be gilded flakes were falling where lances of radiance struck and splintered against treetop shields.

Brad busied himself with a guy rope.

"Brad," I said, starting to roll up the sleeping bags.

"Yes?"

"I'm still here, too. I'll always be here."